A Chronicle of Our House

A Chronicle of Our House

Compiled by Merilyn Mohr

Camden House

CAMDEN
•HOUSE•
PUBLISHING

Canadian Cataloguing in Publication Data

Mohr, Merilyn
    A chronicle of our house

Bibliography: p.
ISBN 0-920656-75-7

1. House construction.   2. Dwellings—Remodelling.
I. Title.

TH4811.M63   690'.837   C88-094514-1

Trade distribution by
Firefly Books
3520 Pharmacy Avenue, Unit 1-C
Scarborough, Ontario
Canada M1W 2T8

Printed in Canada for
Camden House Publishing
(a division of Telemedia Publishing Inc.)
7 Queen Victoria Road
Camden East, Ontario
K0K 1J0

Designed by
Linda J. Menyes

Printed and bound in Canada by
D.W. Friesen & Sons Ltd.
Altona, Manitoba

Printed on 100-lb. Friesen Matte

Contents

Archives

A History of Our House	10
Memories and Milestones	22

A Profile of Our House

Plans and Specifications	36
Photo/Finishes	44
Systems	66

Metamorphosis

Indoor	78
Outdoor	92

For the Record

Maintenance	104
Money Matters	114
Sources	120

Our House

Address _____

The date we take possession _____

We name our house _____

A *Chronicle of Our House* is based on the belief that for most people, a house is not just a careful conglomeration of bricks and beams, concrete and wallboard. It is more like a member of the family. The attachment that people have to the places in which they live is evident in their reluctance to refer to a house by its impersonal street address; instead, a house is often christened, either formally with a name like Bellevue House or informally with a family nickname like Windy Willows or with a community designation like The Old Elston Place. And rightly so. Your house not only shelters you, it is a large part of your life, the backdrop against which memories are made.

This *Chronicle* is designed, therefore, as more than just a place to list the vital statistics of a building. It is a photograph album, a scrapbook and a journal combined, a book where you can record the history of your house and the circumstances of its birth, the changes it undergoes while you make it your home and the details of its structural and working parts. Like the baby book that commemorates a child's early years, this promises to become a family treasure that will be passed along with the property to your heirs, one that will spark reminiscences long after you have moved away. The book is also designed, however, to serve as a practical reference while you live in the house. As you fill in the graphs and charts on these pages, you will create a unique operator's manual for your house that will help you locate hidden wiring and plumbing, match the colour and the kind of paint in the kitchen, and remember the name of the talented, inexpensive carpenter who built those shelves in the family room five years ago.

The New Owners

Our names and ages _____

_____

_____

The first part of the book is a personal architectural archive, a place to preserve the history and memorabilia of your house. The second is a graphic snapshot of the house as it exists when you move in—floor plans of the interior, diagrams of wiring, plumbing and heating systems, and records of the finishes used in each room. This information will prove indispensable when you begin the inevitable alterations that custom-fit a house to its new owners. The third section of the book documents these transformations to both the inside and the outside of the house: why you added the greenhouse, who poured the floor and how well the caulking worked—memory-evoking details that will also prevent you from repeating mistakes. The back of the book is reserved for maintenance charts and financial records, data that will be as useful to subsequent owners of the house as it is to you: how much the house costs to heat, when chemical pesticides were last used, how often the chimney needs to be cleaned. It closes with an extended reading list that covers matters of common household concern.

A Chronicle of Our House is interspersed with anecdotes, quotes and pertinent facts about houses, but most of the book is blank, waiting to be written by its true author, the homeowner. The more diligent you are about pasting in pictures and wallpaper swatches and taking the time to jot down the details of your heating system and your own anecdotes about the day the stone patio was laid, the more you will be rewarded with a book that is not only a valuable reference manual but a cherished chronicle of the years you share with this house.

When Mary came out of this place, she always felt as if she were passing through barricades. The house and its surroundings were so self-sufficient, with their complicated and seemingly unalterable layout of vegetables and flowerbeds, apple and cherry trees, wired chicken run, berry patch and wooden walks, woodpile, a great many roughly built dark little sheds, for hens or rabbits or a goat. Here was no open or straightforward plan, no order that an outsider could understand; yet what was haphazard, time had made final. The place had become fixed, impregnable, all its accumulations necessary, until it seemed that even the washtubs, mops, couch springs and stacks of old police magazines on the back porch were there to stay.

Mary and Danny walked down the road that had been called, in Mrs. Fullerton's time, Wicks Road, but was now marked on the maps of the subdivision as Heather Drive. The name of the subdivision was Garden Place, and its streets were named for flowers. On either side of the road the earth was raw; the ditches were running full. Planks were laid across the open ditches, planks approached the doors of the newest houses. The new, white and shining houses, set side by side in long rows in the wound of the earth. She always thought of them as white houses, though of course they were not entirely white. They were stucco and siding, and only the stucco was white; the siding was painted in shades of blue, pink, green and yellow, all fresh and vivid colours. Last year, just at this time, in March, the bulldozers had come in to clear away the brush and second growth and great trees of the mountain forest; in a little while, the houses were going up among the boulders, the huge torn stumps, the unimaginable upheavals of that earth. The houses were frail at first, skeletons of new wood standing up in the dusk of the cold spring days. But the roofs went on, black and green, blue and red, and the stucco, the siding; the windows were put in, and plastered with signs that said, Murray's Glass, French's Hardwood Floors; it could be seen that the houses were real. People who would live in them came out and tramped around in the mud on Sundays. They were for people like Mary and her husband and their child, with not much money but expectations of more; Garden Place was already put down, in the minds of people who understood addresses, as less luxurious than Pine Hills but more desirable than Wellington Park. The bathrooms were beautiful, with three-part mirrors, ceramic tile and coloured plumbing. The cupboards in the kitchen were light birch or mahogany, and there were copper lighting fixtures there and in the dining ells. Brick planters, matching the fireplaces, separated the living rooms and halls. The rooms were all large and light and the basements dry, and all this soundness and excellence seemed to be clearly, proudly indicated on the face of each house—those ingenuously similar houses that looked calmly out at each other, all the way down the street.

Today, since it was Saturday, all the men were out working around their houses. They were digging drainage ditches and making rockeries and clearing off and burning torn branches and brush. They worked with competitive violence and energy, all this being new to them; they were not men who made their livings by physical work. All day Saturday and Sunday they worked like this, so that in a year or two there should be green terraces, rock walls, shapely flowerbeds and ornamental shrubs. The earth must be heavy to dig now; it had been raining last night and this morning. But the day was brightening; the clouds had broken, revealing a long thin triangle of sky, its blue still cold and delicate, a winter colour. Behind the houses on one side of the road were pine trees, their ponderous symmetry not much stirred by any wind. These were to be cut down any day now, to make room for a shopping centre, which had been promised when the houses were sold.

And under the structure of this new subdivision, there was still something else to be seen; that was the old city, the old wilderness city that had lain on the side of the mountain. It had to be called a city because there were tramlines running into the woods, the houses had numbers, and there were all the public buildings of a city, down by the water. But houses like Mrs. Fullerton's had been separated from each other by uncut forest and a jungle of wild blackberry and salmonberry bushes; these surviving houses, with thick smoke coming out of their chimneys, walls unpainted and patched and showing different degrees of age and darkening, rough sheds and stacked wood and compost heaps and grey board fences around them—these appeared every so often among the large new houses of Mimosa and Marigold and Heather Drive—dark, enclosed, expressing something like savagery in their disorder and the steep, unmatched angles of roofs and lean-tos; not possible on these streets, but there.

Alice Munro, from "The Shining Houses"

We shape our buildings, then our buildings shape us.   Winston Churchill

Archives

A History of Our House
Memories and Milestones

Home is where the heart is.   Pliny

Every house has a history, though the genealogy of a newly minted condominium will be a far cry from that of a Victorian farmhouse. If you have built your own house, use the following pages to record the triumphs and tribulations of the construction process, from buying the land and choosing a design to driving the last finishing nail. You will have to be selective to condense this epic event into a concise 20-page tale, but friends and relatives will thank you for sparing them from shuffling through thick decks of photographs that are meaningful only to the principal players in your house-building saga. Choose the most evocative photographs, and fill in the blank spaces with anecdotes about the near-hurricane that almost crumpled the frame, the crusty neighbour who unerringly divined the underground spring and the party that marked the closing in of the shell.

If you are not the first owner of the house, the details of its past may be more elusive. Question the people who sold you the house about its background; they may already have documented its history. At the very least, they will be able to elaborate on the changes they have made to the structure during their sojourn and they may even give you copies of photographs of the house as it was when they bought it. Digging for Documents will help you trace the ancestry of the house further. If you fail to unearth pictures of the house in its original condition, use these pages as a scrapbook for photocopies of historical documents and news clippings about previous owners. It might be wise to wait until most of the research is complete before filling in this section so that you are certain to have room to tell the whole story. Instead of writing on the actual page, consider fastening in a typewritten biography of the house that could be amended as you unravel the colourful details of your house's past.

The history of the house might not be as interesting as that of the property it stands on. Even a brand-new subdivision house that was bought ready-made is built on land that has a history stretching back before humankind. Local history books will be able to tell you if Blackfoot camped here every summer or if Fenians first farmed the site, and some research into local geology may reveal that you live on the beach of a sprawling prehistoric lake. Or you may decide to use this section to record only your association with the house, pasting in the newspaper ads that first alerted you to the property and recounting your first impressions on touring the house and the details of your decision to buy.

Whether your house is new or new-to-you, it is part of a community. In the city, it might be as small as a single street or a few blocks; in the country, it might expand to include a 40-square-mile township or a mountainside. In the final two pages of this part of your personal archives, draw a map of the world that surrounds your house, identifying the neighbours' houses, local hangouts like the corner store, the library and the school playground, and the landmarks that are part of your weekly ritual, like the bakery that sells fragrant, dark pumpernickel on Saturdays or the farm where you buy your free-range eggs. As the neighbourhood—and your small part of it—evolves, you will have a lasting record of how it was.

Phileen Dickinson

Digging for Documents

When Joyce Devlin bought the ramshackle one-and-a-half-storey house on the main street of Merrickville, Ontario, she knew it was old, but it took some sleuthing to piece together the building's genealogy. The house was built of limestone laid up in rough courses, one half exposed, the rest hidden under stucco. This proved an important clue: rubblestone was widely used in early 19th-century house construction, but because it was considered inferior to uniform, cut blocks of stone, it was often covered. Forty years later, standards changed, and the stone was allowed to stand on its own merits. The off-centre front door, large windows, low roof pitch and solid rectangular design of the stuccoed section are Georgian, while the steeper roof angle, tall narrow windows and gable on the stone half of the house are typically Gothic. A Rumford fireplace buried behind a plaster wall firmly establishes the Georgian half of the house as circa 1830, the year that a tax on fireplaces made cast-iron stoves the norm. Taken together, these disparate elements indicate that Devlin's house was originally built between 1825 and 1835, probably as a simple workman's cottage, and expanded with a stone addition between 1860 and 1880.

House Hieroglyphs

Architectural details and construction techniques are the hieroglyphs in which the story of a house is written. Translated correctly, the curve of the verandah posts and slope of the roof can reveal the approximate birth date and structural evolution of a house, but because building styles are not adopted and abandoned as quickly and universally as clothing fads, this is accurate only to within a decade or two. Furthermore, the alterations of successive owners may completely obscure the true origins of a house: a stark farmhouse, stripped of its telltale bargeboards and balconies, may bear little resemblance to the Victorian mansion that was originally built.

Inside Information

Sometimes, the inside is more revealing than the exterior profile of a house. Styles of trim and floorboards can be giveaways, though the most telling clues are usually found in the attic and basement, the rooms that are least tampered with. Here, exposed structural members may indicate the age of the house, though relying on this evidence is risky since building materials were often recycled, the beams from a neighbour's storm-toppled barn serving as joists for a new house. Fasteners, however, were rarely reused and thus may provide credible clues to the original construction of a house. The local historical society or architectural preservation group should be able to refer you to an expert who can read the history of your house in its nails, hinges and door latches.

Still, without an actual cornerstone, the birth date of the house will not likely be found in the structure itself: an accurate genealogy can only be compiled by sifting through private memories and public records. The local Women's Institute or historical society is a good place to start. Many have published books that trace the histories of local landowners, and if you are lucky, you may glimpse your house behind the stiffly smiling faces of family portraits. Talk to your neighbours and elderly people who have spent their lives in the community. When you know the names of previous occupants, you can visit the library to consult old newspapers and telephone and street directories. You may discover that the house was once a doctor's office or a buggy repair shop, since these directories often included the occupation of the resident.

Deeds and Records

Much of the information about a house is in the public domain. Property tax records, available from the municipal tax assessment office, may show the date of construction, previous owners, recent building permits and even the structure of the house, with a rough sketch of its original dimensions. The deed to the property is also an important source of information. Deeds tell you names, dates and prices, and at the land titles department of the county or city registry office, you can search through previous owners' deeds to find the original owner—and thus the original date—of the house. Finally, the municipal building department, which maintains records of building permits, may yield information on structural changes to the house: the date of alterations, the name of the architect, the cost of construction and perhaps even floor plans. This search may prove fruitless, however, since in some localities building permits have only been required for a few decades, and even today, alterations are often undertaken without official blessing.

Photo Research

Once the resources of the library and municipal offices have been exhausted, you can broaden your search. Some cities keep photographs on file of early architecture and streetscapes. If you know the name of a prominent local photographer who worked at the time your house was built, check city and provincial archives and libraries for collections of his work. The older the building, the more challenging this architectural sleuthing becomes. Not everyone will choose to unravel the tale, but knowing a building's past makes it a more interesting place to live and affects your own contributions to its continuing evolution. With a little research, future renovations can be designed to enhance—not detract from—the architectural legacy of your house.

Photo Diary

The date our house was built _____

Who built our house _____

Legal description of the property _____

Where our deed is filed _____

Photo Diary

Photo Diary

One of the greatest pleasures of life is to build a house for one's self . . . . I notice how eager all men are in building their houses, how they linger about them, or even about their proposed sites. When the cellar is being dug, they want to take a friendly hand in it; the earth evidently looks a little different, a little more friendly and congenial than other earth. When the foundation walls are up and the first floor is rudely sketched by rough timbers, I see them walking pensively from one imaginary room to another, or sitting long and long, wrapped in sweet reverie, upon the naked joist.

John Burroughs

Photo Diary

Photo Diary

Photo Diary

Photo Diary

Eighteen months before the wedding, my mother had eyed my father's bachelor shack with ill-disguised disgust. It was a single room with a one-slant roof, a bare-boards parallelogram rising stark and ugly from the grass.

"Jack, I can't live in that—that *thing*!" she said. "I want a proper house."

"Of course you want a proper house, and a proper house you shall have!" he cried extravagantly. "Just draw me a picture of what you'd like."

She sketched a charming one-storey frame building with an attic dormer, a big bay window and a shady east verandah. Like every other prairie person of his time, my father then turned to Timothy Eaton's mail-order catalogue for comfort and advice. It was a personal thing, the bond between customers and Mr. Eaton. Although Timothy was already dead a dozen years, my parents and their neighbours invariably addressed him by name: "Well, let's see what Timothy Eaton's got on sale this time."

In 1919, Timothy's main catalogue offered B.C. salmon at 15¢ a tin, bacon at 38¢ a pound, genuine dogskin coats for $34.50 and the ever-popular "Venus de Milo front-lace corset with famous Flex-o-steel boning" at $3.75. His supplementary Soldiers' Settlement catalogue held all the farm machinery a veteran could ever want. Most important, Timothy's Building Supplies catalogue sold *complete* houses: lumber, paint, hardware, nails, the exact amounts needed for each of nearly a dozen house plans. One of them was Modern Home #663, "designed especially for young housekeepers—beginners in matrimony."

What luck! They were beginners in matrimony—and #663 was almost identical to my mother's sketch. Just one problem: the material alone cost $883.81. My father didn't have it. Nor did he have horses, cows, chickens, ploughs, cultivators, hay mower, barn, granaries, any of the hundred-and-one essential bits of farming paraphernalia.

A cautious man would have given up, but not a Brian O'Lynn. He took out a 3-thousand-dollar mortgage on his land, although he loathed debt. At a time when the finest tweed suit cost only 12 dollars, 3 thousand dollars was a crushing burden. He bought the lumber and gave Mother's sketch and the page from Eaton's catalogue to a local handyman. Up went the house. It took him 23 years to pay off the mortgage, but he begrudged not a penny of it.

He was an incurable romantic. He set the house just so, on a little hill with its face to the sun and its back to the north winds. At 30 feet long by 20 feet wide, it was

no bigger than a rich man's recreation room, but he fenced a 10-acre surrounding yard, a grand estate that made up for the modest dimensions within.

By autumn 1920, it was ready, although never to be finished according to plan. Year after year, if the crops didn't fail the price of grain did. Spare cash went for human and animal survival. Little luxuries were put off until "next year." Next year never came.

The house was painted just once, white with green trim. Soon the wind and rain and snow buffed and scoured it to silver grey. Indoors, the plan for plastered walls gave way to heavy paper pasted over boards and tinted with calcimine, a cheap, watery wall colouring.

My father banked barnyard manure around the foundation each autumn. The stink faded after a while, the snow-covered manure kept drafts from under the floors, and the rotted remains made excellent garden mulch in the spring. But the walls were not insulated and on winter nights when the Fahrenheit thermometer dipped to 30 below zero, the living room coal stove glowed like the hubs of hell while the bedrooms 10 feet away were as frigid as Axel Heiberg Island. White polka dots of frost grew thick on the exposed nail heads. Frost jungles and palm trees twirled and swirled on the windowpanes.

For years the verandah went without a floor. But there was a real brick chimney, when many other settlers were content with a tin smokestack. And the attic was *almost* everything he dreamed of. On the January night in 1920 when he brought his bride home, he stopped her in the snowy yard. "Wait, don't go inside! Not yet! Wait here and watch!"

Then he trotted a kerosene lantern up a ladder into the attic to proudly show how light shone golden through the four dormer windows. It would never be more than a storage place and a hideout for small boys, but it gave the little house a touch of class.

And in this house one September evening I was born. It had been a crisp, amber Wednesday with goldenrod flooding the ditches and wheat standing ripe in the stook and the pasture tinged with autumn yellow. My father came in early from the fields and my mother said, "I think it's time. Better call Dr. Woodside." . . . Dr. Woodside arrived later to commend all participants. My birthplace was duly registered—not a village or town as for ordinary folk but "Section 10, Township 13, Range 5, West of the 3rd Meridian." I was born on the land, with the land, bonded forever to that land, that little house.

My father got busy and finished the verandah floor.
    Robert Collins, from "West of the 3rd Meridian"

The Neighbourhood

The Neighbourhood

House names predate numbers, which became standard practice only in the mid-1700s when the British post office began delivering mail to individual residences. Houses are often named after the family, the region or natural features such as trees or birds. But folklore also provides inspiration: Valhalla, the Norse warriors' paradise, is a favourite worldwide. The most interesting names, however, have personal significance. Captain James Harris named his Oakville, Ontario, house Benares after the city in India where he served in the 24th Foot Regiment; the stone house is better known today as Jalna, the site of Mazo de la Roche's 15-novel series about the Whiteoaks family. Sculptor Robert Tait McKenzie's house, the Mill of Kintail, was named after the family stronghold in the Scottish Highlands. The log cabin behind poet Earle Birney's family homestead in Banff, Alberta, is less obscure; its name is carved above the door: Kwitcherkik-in.

The day you move into your house is more than the transposition of possessions from one shelter to another. It is a journey that winds both forward and back, a beginning to a new phase of your life and a wistful time of recollection as you convey the stuff you couldn't bring yourself to throw out—the three-legged table you bought at the auction for $10, the God's-eye wall hanging you gave each other for your anniversary, the scrapbooks and albums of people and events recalled only on moving days.

Moving day is the first milestone you will mark in your house. Although not directly involved with the house in any structural way, events like bringing home the baby, planting a tree on her first birthday and hosting the family reunion are all integrally connected to the place you call home. This section of your archives is reserved for just such occasions, played out against the backdrop of your house.

Begin by recording the highlights of moving day.

Within the first few weeks, set down your initial impressions of living in the house. The space will soon become familiar and the things that seemed most pressing to change—the low afternoon light in the living room, the cupboard door that opens the wrong way— will fade into familiarity. Use page 26, Hopes and Dreams, to record your wish list for the house, perhaps even drawing a sketch or pasting in a picture that illustrates how you would like to transform it. Consider leaving a space for a photograph of the house as it looks when you move out. Use the remaining seven pages to record significant family events and natural phenomena that affect the house: the Super Snowstorm of 1992 that heaped drifts to the windowsills and the Flash Flood of 2003 that swamped the basement for 11 days. This personal archive is a diary of your years in this house: the few moments it takes to paste in pictures and news clippings and jot down a tale or two will be repaid with years of rich recollections.

I call the place ''my'' cottage or, when I remember that what is mine also belongs to my wife and children, ''our'' cottage: but it has sad, pleasant ghosts, and there are respects in which it will never be entirely ours. Not ghosts really, for the people who were here are still alive. They just won't be coming back. We bought the place a couple of summers ago, and there was a hot day when the old man and the old woman came out here for the last time. There were a few things they wanted to take back to their place in the city, and the old man, who was correct in everything I saw him do, wanted to make sure I knew about the tools, and the storm shutters, and the fact that occasionally it was a good idea to spread a bit of tar paper on the roof. The old woman told my wife how good the place had been for their children. She sat outside, where it was not so hot and you could hear the lake flopping on the shore, and she drank some tea from a cup she used how many times before? Perhaps a thousand. The flies bothered her, and she looked as though she might cry. He walked for a while near the water, then they hoped we would be as happy here as they had been, and they left, and we all went swimming.

They left and the place was ours, the poplars, the pines, the big willows that grow in the sand, the hornets and rabbits, and the toads in the long grass, the orange butterflies, and the distant birds of the water. The lace doilies on the arms of the mud-coloured chesterfield were ours, too, and so were the brown, tough wicker chairs; the dining-room table, a darker brown, round, ugly, out of Eaton's in the 1920s, as serviceable as these four tubular metal bed frames; the flannelette sheets and embroidered pillowslips; the odd tumblers that had survived ancient Augusts and look now as though only toothbrushes belonged in them; the grass whip and the lawn mower; the red rubber flyswatter; the profusion of rusty hardware; an old sailbag and a bent splicing fid; the remarkably graceful wooden-handled screwdriver, the pipe wrenches; and hundreds of other glass

or metal or china or cloth or paper things that were not quite our style, and spoke of sunburns we have never felt, raspberry jam we had never tasted, faces we will never know, and nights on which we did not stay up late to sing.

The piano is gone from the cottage but the piano bench is still here, black and significant, and it holds so much evidence of irrevocable pleasure that it makes me think old cottages may be the greatest untapped repositories of social history in the country. When families move from house to house they take all their junk with them, throw it out, or give it away. They leave stuff in a cottage because they've always left stuff there to use again when the winter has passed, and because there isn't any other place where it so truly belongs.

The birdbath is gone from the lawn, smashed by strangers who did not care how many summers it had stood there. I've built a crude bench in the grass, out of heavy planks that had washed up on the shore, and another bench from the big poplar that fell in a storm only this month. We've painted the pea-green walls white, and the grey floorboards a deep red. We've taken down the photograph of the nearby lighthouse as it looked on some wild winter afternoon, and the shadowy brown one of an old, small airplane with the pilot's head sticking up in the open breezes of a lost sky. We've put up our own pictures, bright photographs from magazines, and those children's drawings that only their parents can love. The place is becoming ours, but I still can't throw out the stuff in the piano bench because, even if the big poplar did fall down, the sound of the wind in the trees is the same as it must have been 35 years ago, and the water moves as it did then, and as I've learned from my recent studies of ''When I Grow Too Old to Dream'': ''After you've gone, life will go on, Time will be ten-der-ly melt-ing our tears.''

Harry Bruce, from ''Ghosts of Summers Past''

Moving Day

The day we moved in _____

The friends who helped _____

_____

Moving Day

First Impressions

When I bought my farm, I did not know what a bargain I had in the
bluebirds, bobolinks, and thrushes.

Ralph Waldo Emerson, 1862

Hopes and Dreams

If I were asked to name the chief benefit of the house, I should say:
the house shelters day-dreaming, the house protects the dreamer.

Gaston Bachelard

Family Events and Natural Phenomena

Family Events and Natural Phenomena

The owner should bring honour to the house, not the house to the owner.

Cicero, 45 B.C.

Family Events and Natural Phenomena

Family Events and Natural Phenomena

Family Events and Natural Phenomena

Family Events and Natural Phenomena

Family Events and Natural Phenomena

To one who genuinely loves houses—both inside and out—there is no occupation so fascinating as restoring a once beautiful house that has been maimed, or discovering the possibilities in one of seemingly hopeless ugliness.

Emily Post

In the driveway, there is a plain van parked with its blunt hood nosing into the street and its rear doors open wide. I turn the living room light off and see a man with bushy hair and a beard, illuminated by a street lamp, hauling a propane tank half his own size from the dark interior of the van. I try to read his licence plate (evidence if I need it), but without leaving the house with a flashlight and brushing the snow from it, I can't make out the number. The man, now from the side window, walks the propane tank up the driveway as if he knew the house intimately. (Then I remember that the delivery receipt handed me by the oil company truck driver always has *A côté du garage* written somewhere on it.) Through a rear window, I can see the man hunched over the snow-buried path that the oil line follows between the tank and the house. A red glow from the torch appears and becomes a watery pastel as the light haloes his head and shoulders. He works without moving his body except to sweep the oil line with the broad red flame from his torch. Then the flame shrinks, and he drops the torch in the snow and walks through the backyard (more intimacy!) to my side door. Both my wife and I jump at the sound of his knock.

His bush of hair turns out to be an oil-darkened parka but his beard is real enough and even though the house is freezing inside, his beard is still dripping moisture from the heat of the torch. He asks if I will turn the heat up to 85 degrees and take him to the furnace. His English is at that rudimentary stage which makes both speaker and listener feel backward, and he ends each of his sentences with *la*, pronouncing the word so that it almost sounds as if he is saying "low."

I turn the heat up at the thermostat, and he follows me to the basement, where he opens the furnace fuse box and slams it shut, slides the cover from a grey metal box attached to a round, galvanized duct that seems to pierce the combustion chamber itself, and heavily pushes the flat red reset button.

The furnace makes a sound like a very heavy animal beginning to move after a long hibernation. Two ejaculatory bursts of flame shine out the inspection window and briefly turn the repairman's face red as he peers inside. The flame catches and the furnace shakes the walls with its roar. A warm, greasy smell fills the air.

"*Ça marche, la,*" he announces.

We stand at opposite ends of the laundry room, a basket of dirty clothes between us. I feel at ease with working men and their own mysteries—partly because they all seem eager to explain what they're doing and to teach you all they can, undiscovered stars all—and offer him a cup of tea, which he accepts with the pleased surprise that they always do. When I bring the cup downstairs for him, he is once again squatting in front of the inspection window. Seeing me, he stands up and announces that I should switch to stove oil for the coldest months of winter (which I've done in the past, but it still doesn't prevent the accumulated condensation from freezing the valve) and that I should pour in a couple of gallons of *alcool* to absorb the moisture in the line (something new). Then he tells me that he's been working for 15 hours straight and grins wearily through his glistening wet beard.

"I don't mind in the winter," he says. "We are living our lives very easily, *la*. In the north, the, uh, *trappeurs, la*, they are living much colder than us."

He describes how he and his brother and their wives camped in a snowy Laurentian pass for two weeks and drove back home with the car windows cranked all the way down because they were so used to the cold. He says they could feel the heat from the city when they were still 25 miles away. He slurps his dark, unsweetened tea, sounding like he's straining it through his front teeth. My wife has given us china cups, and I can see the oil stains his fingers are leaving on the handle. We both seem to have already run out of things to say to each other.

But he has only been planning his sentences before speaking them. "Since 10 millions of years," he says, "everything that was living on the earth is dead. It goes under the ground and . . ." The word completely escapes him. "It turns into the oil, *la*." Then he taps my scrawny copper feed line. "We are burning everything that was alive. In 10 million years, the people alive now are going to heat up some guy's house, *la*," he says, opening his mouth wide and laughing.

The sound of the furnace resonates dimly through our house, and we can still see our breath, hesitant little puffs, if we wander too far from the warm kitchen. We are both exhausted. When I paid the repairman and saw him to the door, I felt something new in the outside air, perhaps a wearing down of the season. Back in the kitchen, I found my wife nodding asleep, the high colour of her cheeks gone. Awake now, she sniffs at the oily air, and I wonder if I should open a window to let it out. Instead, I take my wife in my arms and let her fall back to sleep while the furnace motor, humming below us, sounds the relentless countdown to spring.

Terence Byrnes, from "Wintering Over"

A house is a machine for living in.   Le Corbusier

A Profile of Our House

Plans and Specifications
Photo/Finishes
Systems

Your house is your larger body.   Kahlil Gibran

Archives captures the spirit of your house, its architectural past and its human history. This section—your house *Profile*—is a thumbnail sketch of the house as it stands when you move in. As a house evolves, it is imperative to have a record of its material substance, its decorative facade as well as its skeletal structure and working parts. This is especially true if you plan to do a historical rehabilitation. Photographs are an instant, accurate and inexpensive record. Supplemented with detailed drawings, they give a graphically clear picture of the house that you have made your home.

If this is a new house, much of the technical data about its construction and finishes will be at your fingertips. In fact, it will be a relief to distil the bulging file of carpet swatches and wiring diagrams into 37 pages arranged room by room for easy reference. Set aside time to translate your construction drawings into simplified floor plans, cross sections and sketches of the mechanical systems of the house. Don't wait too long before filling in this section. You may think your memory will be able to supply the pertinent details about the colour and type of paint and where you bought it, but accurate records will prove more reliable.

If the house is new-to-you, it may be more difficult to fill in some parts of this section. With the help of a measuring tape, you can easily reproduce the floor plans, but until you begin renovations, you may have to rely on the realtor's description for details that are buried in the building envelope. Check the attic and the basement, places where no plaster or wallboard hides the skeleton of the house, for clues about its framing and insulation. Although most of a building's operating systems—electrical wiring, plumbing pipes and heating ducts—snake unobtrusively through walls and ceilings, you can often trace these arteries by a process of deduction. The finishes will be most difficult to track down, both inside and outside the house. Although you will probably want to redecorate to suit your own tastes, knowing what is already on the walls, floors and ceilings is important. Sometimes you can distinguish water- and oil-based paint by sight and touch, but often you don't discover that the kitchen was painted with oil until its new coat of latex paint starts to bubble and peel. If there is a stash of old paint cans in the basement, jot down the types and colours before throwing them out. If not, it may be worth trying to contact the previous owners or taking a chip pried from behind the radiator to the nearest paint store for identification.

Most houses contain kitchens, bathrooms, bedrooms and living rooms, but beyond these basics, there are countless variations in house plans and room designations: the third floor of a two-storey house may be either a basement or a finished attic, and one family's study may be another's den or dining room. Therefore, this section was designed to be as flexible as possible. The site plan and a main-floor plan are labelled, but the other titles remain blank so that you can fill in what is appropriate for your particular design. Likewise, use whatever scale is necessary to fit your house onto these pages. Because this is a technical profile, there is likely little need for personal comment, but should you want to record the impact of the ubiquitous hospital-green paint or the disturbing mix of lead, iron and plastic plumbing pipe, there is plenty of space in the margins.

Phileen Dickinson

Drawing the Lines

Drawing plans is not difficult. To start, you need a good sharp pencil, some 8½-by-11-inch paper and a retractable metal measuring tape. In most houses, the walls intersect at right angles, but if the partitions are oblique, a protractor will also be useful. After taking the measurements, draw the plan to a scale that will fit the page, then transfer it accurately onto the graphed page of the book. You can draw the plans entirely freehand, or for a more formal result, use a steel-edged ruler for the straight lines and French curves or a pencil compass for the arcs. A key to architectural symbols commonly used on house drawings is on page 43.

☐ **Site Plan**

Start with the site plan, a drawing of the outside dimensions of the house and the land that surrounds it. If the building sits on a large acreage, draw only the portion you use as a yard, but include any services connected to the house—telephone or electrical cables, drainage pipes and ditches, the well, the septic system and driveways. Get rough dimensions of your property from the deed, the lot plan or the real estate ad, then map it on the graph to as large a scale as possible. Take the outside dimensions of the house and the distances between the house and the property lines, then draw the house on the site plan, positioning it accurately within the boundaries of the lot. Be sure to include decks, patios and other extensions of the house that are not enclosed living spaces.

If future expansion plans include a sunspace or windows for improved daylighting, mark south on the drawing. While you are making the rough sketch of the site, note the position of trees, gardens and flowerbeds, the size and location of sheds and other outbuildings, and any visible utilities such as telephone lines or well caps. When you draw the finished site plan on page 38, draw in the municipal road allowances and setback lines that govern how close a building can be to the street and to the outside edge of the property.

☐ **Floor Plans**

If the house is new and you have construction plans to work from, drawing the floor plans is simply a matter of transferring the interior layout of each floor from the architectural drawings to the pages of the book and labelling them appropriately. These floor plans should be drawn to scale, showing doors and windows but not dimensions and room fixtures. These will only crowd the picture; add them instead to the individual room plans on pages 46 to 65.

If you do not have original house plans to copy, use the outside dimensions determined earlier to draw a rough outline of the house, and sketch in each room as you measure its length and width; accurately locate door and window openings and draw them as shown in the key. The total inside dimensions will be less than the measured outside dimensions, since the building envelope itself takes up several inches. When the floor plans are complete, choose an appropriate scale and copy them onto pages 39 to 41. If the house has more than three floors of living space, reduce the scale and draw two floors on one page. Note load-bearing walls on the drawing by shading them lightly.

☐ **Cross Sections**

As well as floor plans, you will also want a record of the skeletal structure of your house. This is most easily done by drawing a cross section, a side view that looks as if the house were sliced through from the roof to the basement floor, exposing the multiple layers of materials that make up the building shell. For example, a recently constructed frame house might have a wall cross section showing (inside to outside) ⅝-inch drywall, a 6-mil polyethylene air/vapour barrier, 2-by-6 wood framing filled with fibreglass batt insulation, 2-inch fibreglass sheathing, a spun polyester air barrier, wood strapping and cedar siding. Use the symbols in the key to designate different materials, making sure to label the cross section with the actual dimensions of the material, such as 4-inch or 6-inch batts of fibreglass. To save space, draw small separate cross sections of the foundation wall, above-grade wall and roof. On the specifications page opposite, make a note of the construction materials used—single-glazed, vented or low-E windows, for instance. The information on these two pages may not be easy to determine, but it will prove invaluable both to you and to future occupants.

☐ **Elevations**

Drawing a plan of each room may seem time-consuming, but it will be labour-saving in the long run. Recorded once, accurately, the information will be handy whenever it is needed. Start by measuring the length and width of the floors, noting the exact location and width of doorways. Use a line with an arrowhead at each end to show dimensions. Then sketch each of the four walls: these are called elevations and should be labelled north, south, east or west. Note the height and width of each wall as well as the exact location and dimensions of windows and doors, electrical outlets, plumbing fixtures, registers, radiators or baseboards and telephone jacks. Be accurate: a couple of inches can make a big difference when choosing a window blind. Do not forget to indicate closets and built-in furniture such as bookshelves. Use a broken line of dashes to show walls that are hidden from view. When the rough sketches of a room are complete, draw the five diagrams—one floor plan and four elevations—to scale on the graphed side of the double-page spreads that are devoted to individual rooms.

Site Plan   Scale _____

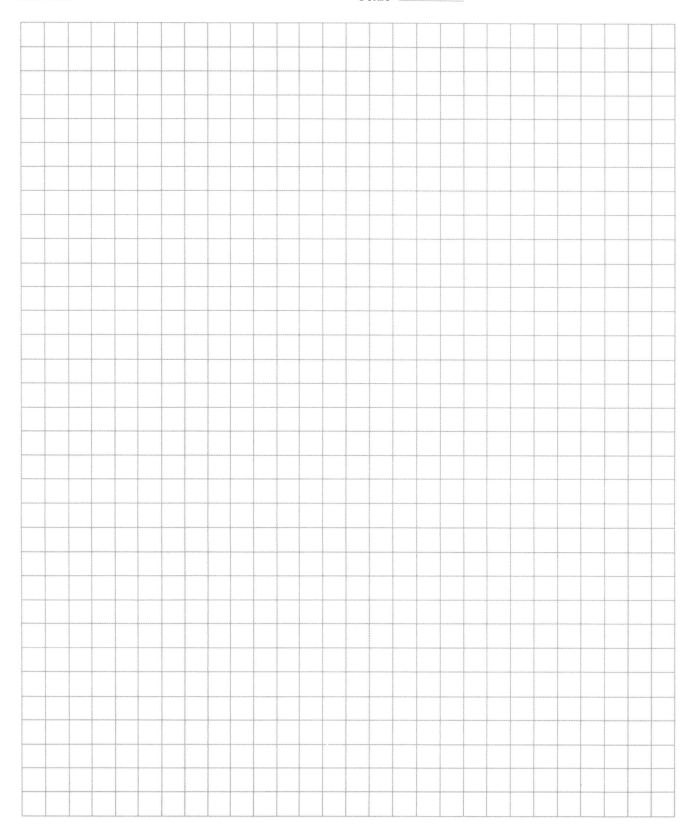

Main-Floor Plan   Scale _____

Floor Plan   Scale

Floor Plan _____   Scale _____

Cross Sections

Material Symbols

batt insulation		drywall	
blown cellulose insulation		siding	or
wood framing		brick	
vapour barrier		concrete	

Material Specifications

Framing: _____

Air/vapour barrier: _____

Sealant: _____

Air barrier: _____

Sealant: _____

R-values: Roof _____

Above-grade walls _____

Foundation walls _____

_____

Exterior doors: _____

_____

Caulking: _____

_____

Windows: _____

_____

_____

_____

Architectural Symbols

dimension lines		toilet	
hidden lines		tub	
window	or	shower	
casement window		sink	or
door (regular)		stove	
(folding)		closets	
(sliding)		heat register	
stairs		fireplace	

This section is a room-by-room profile of your house. Each two-page spread has space for a photograph of the room, drawings of its floor plan and elevations, and a place to record the finishes used. Don't forget to include hallways and entrances; if there is not enough space to record the vital statistics of all the rooms of your house, you can photocopy these pages and add them as inserts.

Use the graphed side of the page to draw a simple floor plan of the room and elevations of the four walls, following the instructions in Drawing the Lines on page 37 and using the symbols on page 43. The scale will vary between the floor plan and elevations, so remember to note it beside each drawing. Do not forget to show built-in furniture and any services—electrical, plumbing, heating, air-conditioning, central vacuum. Ducts in bulkheads or wires and pipes in the walls can be indicated with a dashed line. The exterior only requires elevations; the floor plans are drawn on pages 39 to 41.

Instead of a photograph, you may want to use this space to attach wallpaper, paint or fabric samples. Fill in the section below with details about the finishes: where each was bought, what type of finish it is—including the brand name—the pattern and colour number, when it was applied, how much was used to cover the area and warranty details. You may also want to add comments about how well the paint obscured the previous colour or whether the curtains should be washed or dry-cleaned—anything that will assist you in maintaining and replacing what you use to cover the ceilings, floors, windows and walls. Key the written information to the plans; for instance, number the windows drawn on the elevations, then describe the finishes as window 1, window 2, et cetera. It is a good idea to make these notes in pencil, since they should be updated each time the room is redecorated. If alterations are later made to the room, jot down the page reference here so you can quickly flip between the records of how the room looked before and after.

Exterior Photographs and Swatches

Exterior Elevations

Scale _____

Finishes

Roofing _____

Siding _____

Trim: Soffits and fascia _____

Windows _____

Doors _____

Eaves troughs _____

Deck _____

Fence _____

Porch _____

Driveway _____

Kitchen Plan and Elevations   Scale _____

The first foundation of a good House must be the Kitchin.   Richard Surflet, 1616

Kitchen Photographs and Swatches

Finishes

Floor _____   Windows _____

_____   _____

Ceiling _____   Cabinets _____

_____   _____

Walls _____   Fixtures _____

_____   _____

Trim _____   _____

_____   _____

Living Room Plan and Elevations

Scale _____

It is something to be able to paint a particular picture or to carve a statue, and so to make a few objects beautiful, but it is far more glorious to carve and paint the very atmosphere and medium through which we look . . . . To affect the quality of the day—that is the highest of arts.

Henry David Thoreau

Living Room Photographs and Swatches

Finishes

Floor ....

Ceiling ....

Walls ....

Trim ....

Windows ....

Bathroom Plan and Elevations

Scale _____

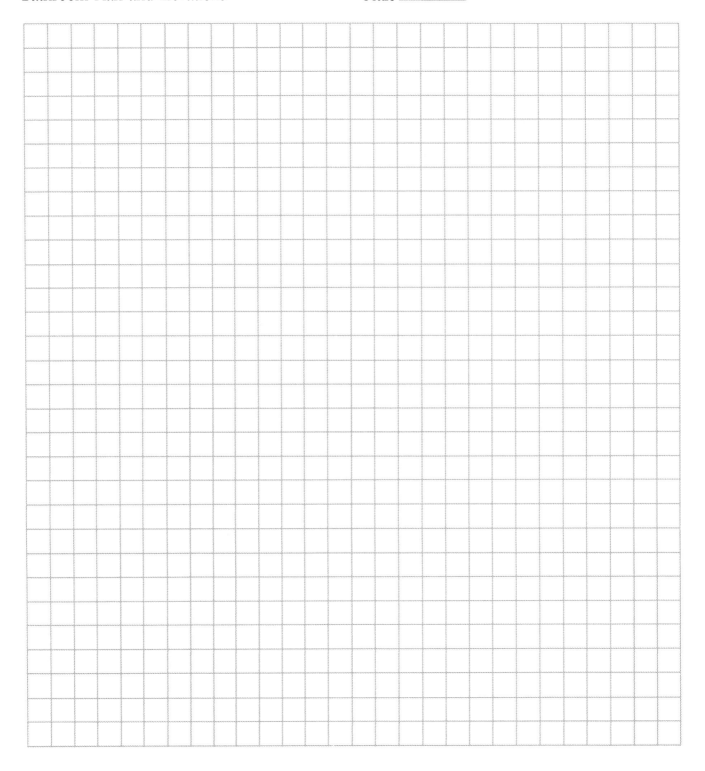

Give me the luxuries of life and I will willingly do without the necessities.

Frank Lloyd Wright

Bathroom Photographs and Swatches

Finishes

Floor	Windows
Ceiling	Cabinets
Walls	Fixtures
Trim	

Bedroom Plan and Elevations   Scale _____

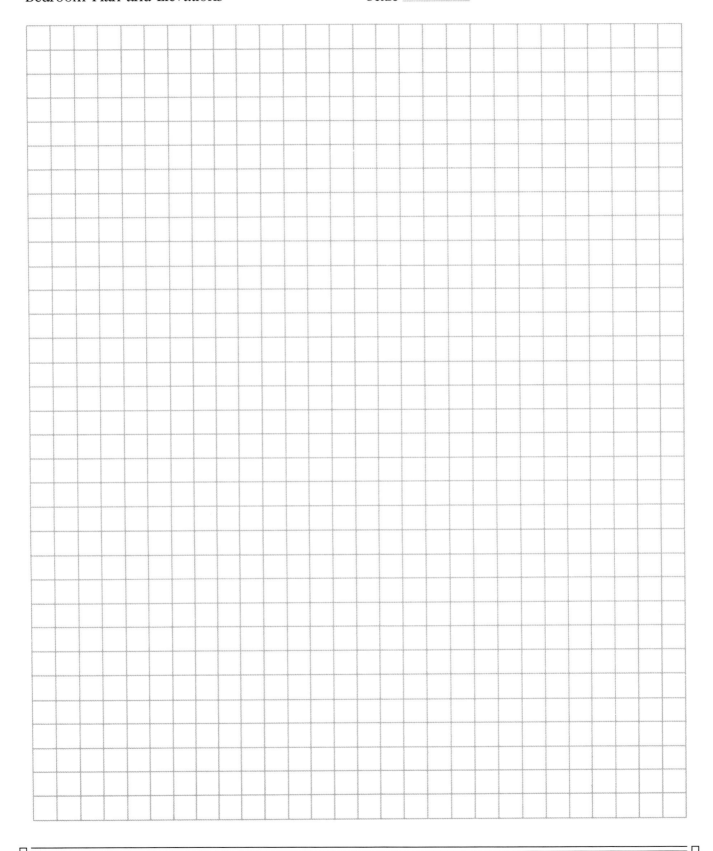

Bedroom Photographs and Swatches

Finishes

Floor _____

Trim _____

Ceiling _____

Windows _____

Walls _____

Photographs and Swatches

Finishes

Floor ....

Trim ....

Ceiling ....

Windows ....

Walls ....

Plan and Elevations   Scale

A white wall is fool's paper.   James Sanford, 1572

Photographs and Swatches

Finishes

Floor ....

Trim ....

Ceiling ....

Windows ....

Walls ....

Plan and Elevations   Scale

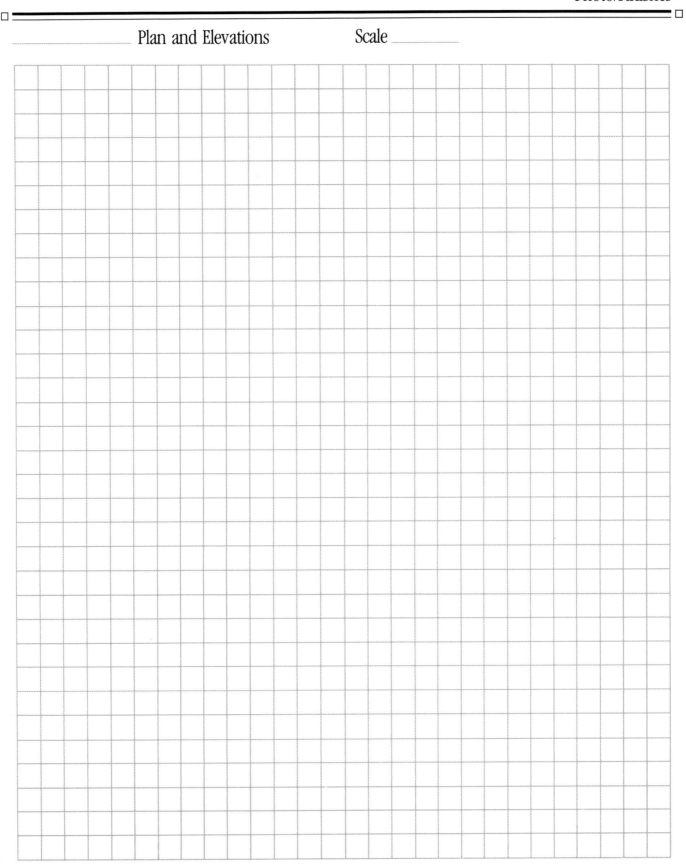

Photographs and Swatches

Finishes

Floor _____

Trim _____

Ceiling _____

Windows _____

Walls _____

Plan and Elevations   Scale _____

Houses are built to live in, and not to look on.   Francis Bacon, c. 1600

Photographs and Swatches

Finishes

Floor

Ceiling

Walls

Trim

Windows

Plan and Elevations   Scale

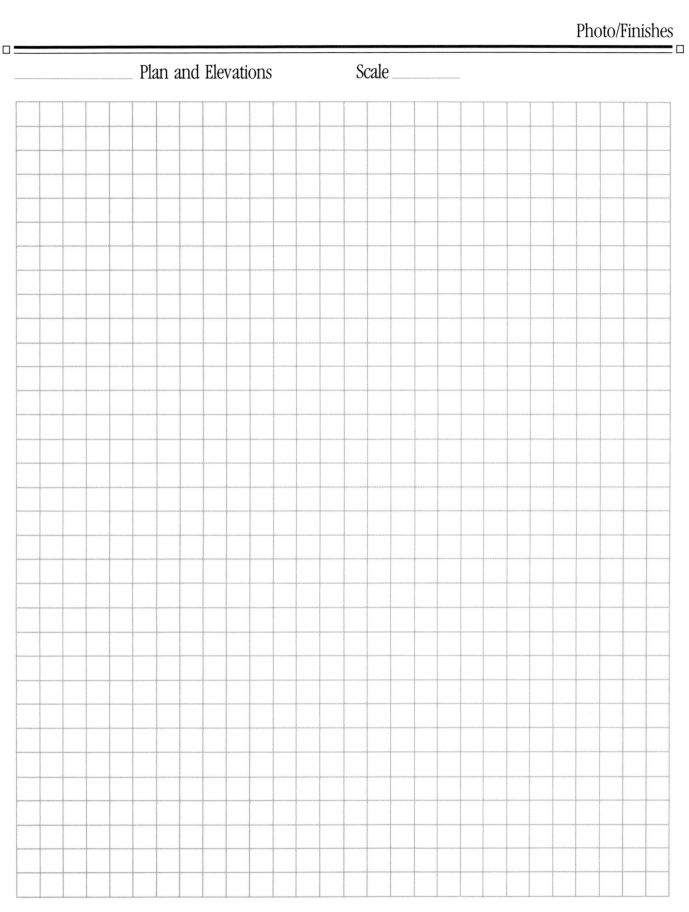

Photographs and Swatches

Finishes

Floor ....

Trim ....

....

....

Ceiling ....

Windows ....

....

....

Walls ....

....

....

Plan and Elevations   Scale _____

Photographs and Swatches

Finishes

Floor _____

Trim _____

Ceiling _____

Windows _____

Walls _____

Plan and Elevations   Scale _____

'Tis joy to him that toils, when toil is o'er,
To find home waiting, full of happy things.   Euripides, 430 B.C.

The House at Work

Central heating systems date back to the early 1800s, but drainage, plumbing and electricity—what Frank Lloyd Wright called the bowels, circulation and nerves of a house—are largely of the 20th century and have evolved remarkably since they were first introduced.

Wiring
No system has had more impact on housing than electricity. In 1880, the first electric light was installed in North America. Within two years, 5,000 electric lamps lit the rooms of more than 200 wealthy homeowners, and by 1900, electric lighting was de rigueur in new houses. It replaced gaslight, which was not only dim but smelly and dirty: much of a housekeeper's time was spent scrubbing glass globes and washing soot off walls and ceilings. But although electricity was originally used for lighting—the first generating plants were called "electric light stations"—it soon found its niche as a power source for mechanical devices that add comfort and convenience to the home. Before World War I, there was an explosion of electrical inventions—the vacuum, refrigerator and sewing machine, to name a few.

The array of electrical labour-saving and entertainment machines continues to grow, making household wiring increasingly complex. In a turn-of-the-century house, wiring was minimal, serving the single overhead bulb that lit each room, but even such a simple installation sometimes posed hidden dangers. Wires were often plastered over, and when the lime ate through the insulative sheathing, there were short circuits and fires. Some electrical "improvements" have been equally disastrous: aluminum wiring, popular in the 1950s, proved to be unsafe when coupled with copper. A wiring inspection by a qualified professional should uncover potential hazards and pinpoint inadequacies. To prevent this silent and invisible servant from becoming a killer, an outdated electrical system should be upgraded to meet current electrical codes.

Plumbing
Plumbing was much slower to invade private homes than electricity. Until the 1800s, human waste was simply deposited in a chamber pot and dumped into the nearest moat or stream. In the city, thundermugs were emptied out the window at assigned waste disposal hours. Although flush toilets date back as far as ancient Rome, the technology was lost during the Dark Ages and only resurfaced a century ago. When indoor plumbing arrived, the toilet was dubbed the "loo," probably a contraction of the lilting "gardyloo"—*garde à l'eau*—which usually preceded the splash of excrement on the street below. Sir John Harington constructed what he called "A Privy of Perfection" near Bath, England, in 1596, but although it incorporated all the elements of the modern flush toilet, the technology did not catch on until just before the Industrial Revolution, when a British watchmaker, Alexander Cummings, patented the first flush toilet in Britain.

The modern bathroom, however, is an American invention, and it was an important innovation in house design. In Britain, the bath was portable and was moved into the dressing room or bedroom as required. The water closet was just that: a closet with plumbing. However, in democratic America, where houses were smaller and there were no servants to haul water to every bedroom, piping it to a single room was more practical. The modest Victorians resisted the idea of communal bathrooms, however, preferring to retain their "pot cupboards"—small cabinets that opened to reveal a seat with a built-in receptacle—rather than share a toilet with other members of the household. Today most new houses have two and sometimes three or four bathrooms, but a recent trend toward an en suite bathroom in every bedroom indicates a curious return to the Victorian predilection for privacy.

Ventilation
The Victorians were also obsessed with fresh air, partly because they believed that many diseases—malaria, cholera and dysentery—were caused by impurities they inhaled. As a result, their high-ceilinged, drafty houses often had air ducts and ventilating flues. The smoky fireplaces that heated these houses were a primary cause of the indoor pollution, but they were considered an important part of the ventilation system, the hole through which stuffy air escaped. In the mid-1800s, fireplaces were gradually replaced with wood- and coal-burning furnaces that ducted warm air from a basement plenum into individual rooms, but there was some resistance to the idea of central heating. In 1850, A. J. Downing wrote in *The Architecture of Country Houses* that "Closed stoves are not agreeable, for they imprison all the cheerfulness of the fireside; and they are not economical, for though they save fuel, they make large doctor's bills." Cleaner heating systems—oil, gas and electricity—removed the emphasis from ventilation, and it is only now, as houses become more airtight in an effort to reduce heating costs, that ventilation systems are regaining importance.

Heating, ventilation, plumbing and wiring systems gave the engineer new prominence in house design. Although they have made houses more comfortable and convenient, the increasing mechanization has also distanced homeowners from the inner workings of their houses since most systems are governed by complex codes and require professional installation. As you sketch in these respiratory, circulatory and alimentary systems, you will have an opportunity to explore and understand a hidden but essential part of your house.

Plumbing

Knowing the plumbing system of your house not only lets you talk intelligently with the plumber, but it may also give you enough confidence to tackle simple repairs yourself.

On the following page, draw a diagram of any outdoor drainage systems. This applies mostly to rural properties and may include a septic bed, a dry well or drainage tile that diverts eaves trough runoff away from the house. The diagram need not be to scale, but it should include specific directions for finding the well cap and the lid to the septic tank. It is especially important to know exactly where the drainfield is located so you don't plant trees or shrubs where their roots will clog the tiles.

On page 69, draw a plumbing diagram for the house. This is tricky, since pipes run vertically as well as horizontally. The best approach is a three-dimensional one—drawing the plumbing as if it were a tree branching off after it enters the house. Alternatively, you can reproduce the floor plans and use them to chart the plumbing routes diagrammatically. To save space, omit rooms without plumbing. A basement plan alone may be sufficient, since the shutoff valves on bathroom and kitchen fixtures are standard: you can find them behind the U-shaped pipe under the sink and behind the toilet bowl, just below the tank.

Start your plumbing diagram by showing the main line that brings water into the house, either from the well or from the municipal water supply. This main line branches off to feed each section of the house, with one branch going directly to the water heater. Risers are pipes that run vertically through the house, feeding fixtures located directly above each other; each branch and riser is fitted with a shutoff valve, usually where it splits off from the main line. Note the location of shut-offs and drain plugs. Draw in the drainage half of the water system, noting drains, waste lines and the stacks, the vertical pipes that vent waste odours. Drainpipes usually have clean-out fittings that can be removed so that you can dislodge clogs. Some of the water lines may be buried in bulkheads or under ceiling tile; if necessary, use a metal detector to trace them. And do not forget outdoor traps. If the drawing becomes too congested, put the plumbing system and drainage system on separate diagrams.

Finally, use the space immediately below to note peculiarities of your plumbing system. Jot down the depth and flow rate of the well and the time of year when water is at a premium. Indicate those crawl space pipes that are prone to freezing during cold snaps and which doors or taps you leave open to keep the water running. Record the season when the sump pump is pressed into service. Most important, make a note of the proper sequence for shutting off and draining the water in your house. Specifics will vary, but in general, the incoming water is shut off, and the pressure tank (if there is one) is drained with a hose. Then the cold-water intake to the water heater is shut and this tank drained. All the fixtures and water-using appliances such as the water heater, washing machine and dishwasher must be drained. All faucets and taps should be opened and toilets flushed to remove water, then mineral oil—not antifreeze—added to the toilet, sink and tub traps to prevent potentially explosive gases from backing out of the septic system into the house. To turn the water back on, the procedure is reversed: close all drains, reconnect all hoses, then open the water supply. When the air has cleared from the system, close the faucets. The mineral oil can safely be flushed into a septic system without causing environmental damage.

Plumbing Peculiarities

_____

_____

_____

_____

_____

_____

Outdoor Drainage

Plumbing Symbols

cold water	————————		hot water	– – – – – –
floor drain	⊠		shower drain	⤬
hot-water tank	(H W)		clean-out fittings	—◁—|

Plumbing Diagram

Beauty commonly produces love, but cleanliness preserves it.   Joseph Addison

Electricity

Wiring is potentially the most dangerous aspect of your house. It is no surprise, then, that its installation is tightly regulated: in both new construction and major renovation, new wiring must be inspected before the walls are closed in as well as after the power is turned on. This is one job that may best be left to professionals. Nevertheless, homeowners should at least know where the electrical services run through the walls, floors and ceilings and which circuits are connected together so that they can avoid inadvertently driving a nail into a live wire or overloading a circuit and risking a fire.

Power may come to your house either above ground or below, buried in a conduit. If the latter is the case, it is important to know exactly where the cable is laid so that you can avoid hitting or crushing it during excavation. Use the space below to draw a simple diagram of the power route from the pole at the road to your house, giving specifics as to how deep the cable is buried and when it was laid. The local utility or previous owners will be able to provide details. Note the location of the electricity meter, and while you are at it, check that it is adequately grounded.

When the power enters the house, it is connected first to the distribution box or electrical panel, where it is divided into the circuits that feed the house. This is where the main switch that shuts off all power to the house is located, as are all the fuses and circuit breakers that control individual circuits. The electrical panels in most newer houses have circuit breakers, switches that trip to the off position when they are overloaded. They only need to be switched on again to restore power. The distribution boxes in older houses usually contain fuses that have to be replaced when they burn out during an overload. The size of the distribution box will depend on the size of the house and the number of circuits required to power it: many older homes have 60-amp service, many smaller houses have 100-amp

service with 24 circuits, and most larger houses and those that are electrically heated have 200-amp service with 42 circuits.

A wiring diagram traces the electrical circuits from the main panel to all rooms of the house. Unless the house is new—in which case a wiring diagram will be available from the electrician—identifying which fuses or breakers govern the dozens of outlets, receptacles and switches in the house will be a challenge. Generally, major electrical appliances—the clothes dryer, water pump, electric stove—have their own individual circuits. With a partner, you should be able to pinpoint these by trial and error: turn each appliance on and have one person stand by it while the other stands at the panel and turns one breaker after the other off. When the controlling breaker is identified, label it. With that breaker turned off, plug a lamp into receptacles in the vicinity and switch on lights in the area to find out if any are on the same circuit as the appliance. Plot what you discover, turn the circuit back on and continue on to the next major appliance. When all the major appliances are plotted, map the rest of the circuits.

On the following pages, reproduce the floor plans of your house and make a simplified wiring diagram of each storey, using the symbols illustrated. Start by drawing the distribution panel, labelling the circuits or fuses alphabetically and applying the same letters to the receptacles, outlets and switches throughout the house. Note the location of major appliances such as clothes dryers, stoves and refrigerators that will not likely be moved. Alternatively, you can use different colours to code each circuit. Do not forget to show wiring in the garage, yard and crawl space. There will also be wiring for furnace thermostats, doorbells, central vacuums, intercoms, exhaust fans and fans for heatilator fireplaces. You may want to include telephone and television cable wiring on the diagram as well.

Service Connections

Wiring Diagram: Main Floor

Scale _____

Wiring Symbols

duplex outlet	⊝		service panel	P
floor outlet	⊙		wires under floor	– – – – – –
outdoor outlet	⊖		wires in wall or ceiling	————
motor	Ⓜ		junction box	Ⓙ
wall switch	S_2		overhead light	⊕
220-volt outlet	⊖ 220		telephone	◂

Wiring Diagram: Scale _____

Content lodges oftener in cottages than in palaces.   Proverb

Wiring Diagram: Scale _____

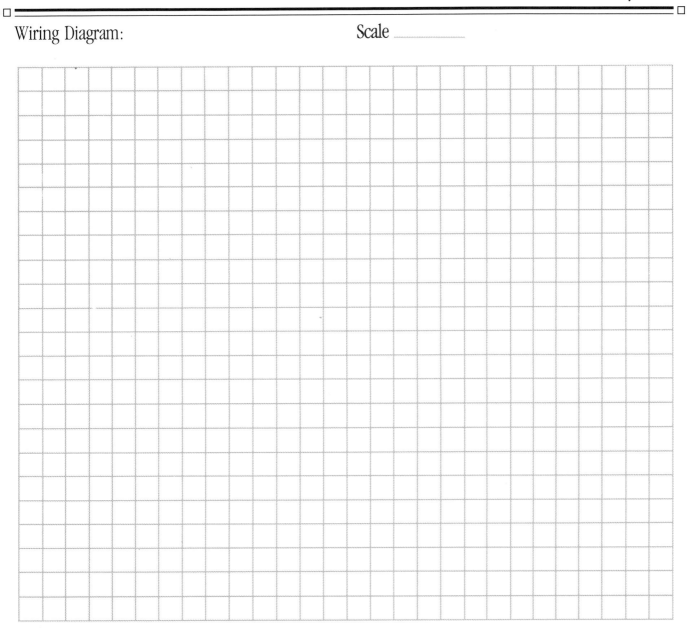

Electricity costs can easily be cut without giving up the pleasures of power. Electrical appliances usually consume about 14 percent of the home energy budget, but this can be reduced by choosing energy-efficient models: for example, a given size of refrigerator/freezer consumes 62 to 165 kwh per month, depending on the manufacturer. It makes sense, therefore, to read energy labels before buying major appliances.

Keeping hot water on tap for dishwashing, laundry and showering accounts for a large proportion of the electrical bill. For an investment of about $50, however, water-heating costs can be cut in half. Most thermostats are set at 160 degrees F, producing scalding water from the tap. Instead, set the thermostat to a usable temperature of 130 degrees, gradually lowering it to 110 degrees if this is acceptable for

washing. If the water heater has two thermostats, keep the upper one about 10 degrees higher. If the tank is an older model, insulate it with a commercially available tank jacket or wrap it with foil-backed fibreglass batts, with the foil side facing out, secured with duct tape. Also, insulate the hot and cold water lines near the hot-water tank, though be sure not to cover the pressure-relief valve on the heater.

Energy-consciousness—turning off lights, radios and televisions when not in use, using cold-water detergent for washing clothes and drying clothes outside when the weather is warm—can help reduce electrical consumption, but so can special conservation devices such as low-energy light bulbs and aerator restrictors that cut water flow from taps by up to 60 percent. These cost little and save a lot without perceptibly affecting the comfort of your house.

Heating, Cooling and Ventilation

The human comfort zone exists within a relatively narrow range of temperature and humidity. Unlike some species, which can live comfortably whether the mercury soars to 90 degrees F or sinks to minus 30 degrees, humans function best when the temperature is between 68 and 80 and when the relative humidity is between 40 and 55 percent. Because the local climate often deviates from this norm, houses are fitted with systems that artificially create a comfortable environment by heating or cooling the space on demand. Many new energy-efficient houses also have mechanical heat-recovery ventilation systems that exhaust stale household air, draw in fresh air and modulate humidity.

These systems do not have to be mechanical. A house can be designed or renovated to include enough south-facing windows to admit passive solar heat to counteract cool outdoor temperatures. Likewise, to cool the house in summer, south-facing windows can be shaded with trees, trellised vines or overhangs, and operable windows can be positioned so that cool summer breezes from the shaded north side of the house waft through the rooms, pushing stale warm air out high windows installed in the south facade. Air vents under the windows can supply fresh air in winter. But in the northern parts of the continent, even the most passive houses usually have some kind of backup heating systems to supplement solar gain and to warm the space on demand in a hurry.

How these pages are filled out will depend on the kinds of systems that heat, cool and ventilate your house. The location of wood stoves, radiant heating panels and exhaust vents can simply be listed. A diagram is more appropriate for systems such as forced-air oil or gas heating, a heat-recovery ventilator or central air conditioner. These mechanicals include duct work that may be hidden in basement bulkheads or buried in the concrete slab floor. Whatever the system, note the location of the heating, cooling or ventilating appliance, pertinent switches, filler pipes, valves and meters, tanks and filters. List instructions for checking fuel levels and for restarting the furnace.

Heating, Cooling and Ventilation

It might be said that the good taste and *savoir-vivre* of the inmates of a
house may be guessed from the means used for heating it.

Edith Wharton and Ogden Codman Jr., 1898

Profile

Fire!

"Early in my experience as an old house enthusiast, I acquired a delightful rubblestone house with barn attached. There were only two rooms downstairs and a large sleeping area above. On the ground floor, covered by panelling and subsequent plaster, was an eight-foot-wide cooking fireplace and adjoining bake oven. Both had obviously been hidden early in the history of the house.

"Needless to say, I was delighted with my discovery. As I removed the rubble from the firebox and oven, I discovered that the flue was absolutely solid with stone, ashes and birds' nests. The astonishing thing was that the house had been heated with a space heater connected to this chimney.

"Over a three-month period I cleaned the flue completely, ending in a mad fit on the roof where I drove a TV aerial up and down in the flue to dislodge the final two feet of debris. The final bit collapsed, a minor explosion of dust poured from windows and doors, but the flue was clear at last. The next two days were spent clearing up the mess in great anticipation of the first fire.

"That first fire was set, very justifiably in my own mind, using lath and debris from the fireplace. With a great sucking sound, the heat was drawn up the chimney. It worked! As I sat in front of it, gleefully throwing on more fuel, I happened to glance out the window. Smoke was everywhere. I ran outside and saw to my dismay that smoke was pouring from every joint in the exterior end wall, culminating in great billows around the soffit and fascia. Inside and upstairs the smoke was doing the same. Miraculously, the house did not ignite. As quickly as possible I extinguished the fire and considered the lesson."

☐ Inspection

As Nigel Hutchins discovered in this tale recounted in his book *Restoring Houses of Brick and Stone*, any heating system, particularly wood-burning stoves and fireplaces, should be inspected for equipment faults, clogged chimneys and disintegrating mortar that allow smoke to spew indoors. There are almost 1,000 house fires every week in Canada; often the difference between a small fire like Hutchins' and one that takes your house or your life is foresight and planning.

As soon as you move into a new house, check it for smoke detectors. House fires usually happen between 10 p.m. and 6 a.m., and most of the victims are not burned to death but suffocate from the poisonous gases that rise ahead of the flames. Smoke detectors are sensitive to minute traces of smoke and may be triggered even when the fire is far away. A smoke detector on each floor or one placed between the bedrooms and the rest of the house will provide adequate protection. If the house already has smoke detectors, check that they work. The batteries in self-contained units must be routinely replaced; check that the fuses are still good for detectors that are wired into the household electrical system.

☐ Escape Plan

Being forewarned of a fire is not enough: you should have an escape plan so you can leave a burning house quickly even if smoke and toxic fumes block the obvious exits. Sit down with your family and map out a complete fire escape plan for every room, then have regular drills so the route is automatic in an emergency.

Stairways and halls are not reliable exits since they often act as funnels for rising heat and toxic gases. If the bedroom door feels cool, open it just a crack; if there is no hot draft, leave by this route. Don't waste time dressing or picking up mementos. Cover your nose and mouth with a wet cloth and crawl to an outside door; the air near the floor is usually clearest. Practise manoeuvring from bedrooms to the outdoors with your eyes closed so you will be able to do it in thick smoke.

If the top of the bedroom door or the knob feels hot, the hall is probably impassable; close the door, and use the windows as exits. Windows in a bungalow are usually safe exits, but in a two-storey house, windows that do not lead to a roof need escape ladders that hook over the windowsill. Buy one for each room and keep it handy, not buried at the back of a closet.

Arrange a place where the family will meet after leaving the building, and decide in advance who will help young children, invalids or the elderly to escape. In a two-storey house, children and older people should sleep in rooms with roof access, since they may have trouble climbing down ladders. Each room should have a window that opens easily and is big enough to crawl through. Learn how to break a window safely using a heavy object, shielding the face from flying glass and removing jagged edges with a shoe before crawling through. Finally, keep the fire department's number handy to all telephones. Better yet, memorize it. It could save your life.

☐ Extinguishers

If you notice a fire in time, you may be able to extinguish it before it threatens your house and family. Every house should have at least one multipurpose fire extinguisher, labelled A for paper, wood and upholstery fires, B for fires in flammable liquids like gasoline, paint and kitchen grease and C for electrical fires. If you buy more than one, install a BC in the kitchen, an A in the living room and an ABC in the basement and garage. Service fire extinguishers regularly and store them near the escape routes of the house so that you can get out quickly if your attempts to control the blaze fail.

Metamorphosis

Indoor Conversions
Outdoor Evolutions

The house praises the carpenter.   Ralph Waldo Emerson

A house never stops evolving. From the moment we buy a house, we begin to make it our own, at first by filling it with our own furniture and paintings, then by peeling the gargantuan gardenias off the bedroom wall and replacing them with diminutive daisies, and finally by knocking out partitions and putting up porches, decks and family-room additions.

Cosmetic or decorative changes—repainting the kitchen or installing a chair rail in the dining room—can be recorded in the previous *Profile* section under Photo/Finishes. Most houses, however, eventually undergo major alterations—adding a dormer to convert the attic to a bedroom, jacking up the house to add a basement or building a sunspace off the living room—designed either to upgrade the structure or to adapt it more precisely to the changing needs of the family.

Metamorphosis is a record of these transformations. Use the chart on pages 80 and 81 to keep track of the technical details of each renovation: when it was started and finished, who did the design and construction, how much the work cost for materials and labour and what went right—and wrong. This will prove helpful in keeping the house adequately insured for its full value and in determining a fair price, should you ever sell the family homestead. The renovation chart is followed by a 10-page diary where you can describe the interior evolution of your house. If you plan to gut the rooms and rebuild everything inside the shell, use the entire section to record the project; otherwise, devote a page or more to an individual alteration. There is plenty of blank space for before and after photographs or diagrams, and you can describe the planning and

execution of the projects in the lined sections.

Alterations to the interior are followed by a record of changes to the outside of the house and to the property—the addition of decks, fences, play equipment and outbuildings. Simple changes in finishes, such as replacing the worn roof shingles with slate tile or covering the stucco with board and batten, should be recorded in the previous chapter. Reserve this part of the book for major construction and reconstruction, such as building a brick courtyard off the family room or replacing precast concrete steps with hand-laid stone.

The last two pages are reserved for landscaping. Use the space to draw a diagram of the yard, noting the names of trees and shrubs and the location of vegetable and flower gardens. The layout of vegetable gardens should rotate regularly, but you can make detailed drawings of perennial beds, including species names and the number of bulbs or plants. This is best done in pencil because it will change slightly from year to year as the landscaping evolves. To avoid too much clutter on the diagrams, number or letter the plants, and label them in the lined space below, noting their flowering habits and watering or cultivation preferences. This will prove helpful in planning future landscaping projects—both for yourself and for subsequent owners of the house—and will be a handy reference when you are giving instructions to someone else to care for the yard.

While you have had the immediate satisfaction of filling in the blanks in *Archives* and *Profile*, *Metamorphosis* will evolve slowly, but it will be a lasting reminder of the permanent mark you leave on your house.

Phileen Dickinson

Making Changes

There was a time when building your own house was common, when putting a roof over your head was not only a practical necessity but an opportunity to express yourself with mortar and stone or log and adze. Built to last, houses were a permanent testament to the builder's skill and a personal legacy to pass on to daughters, sons and their offspring. Today, few families enjoy the luxury of living in the same house generation after generation. People move to where there is work, and families splinter; but it is a mistake to believe that in the process shelter has become just another commodity to use for a time and abandon with little regret.

A recent survey in one Canadian city revealed that the house-building instinct is still strong: although only a small fraction of the homeowners had actually constructed their own dwellings, well over half of the house-buying public said that they would like to. For one reason or another—lack of available land, inadequate skills, job pressures—most never do. Instead, they fulfil their need for a personalized living space by renovating, adding their own special imprint to a house that already exists.

Renovations come in all shapes and sizes, from replacing the over-the-sink slider in the kitchen with a prefab greenhouse window to crowbar conversions that strip a space to its wood-frame shell. But whether large or small, carpenter-built or self-styled, there are certain rules of thumb that can help you get the most for the time and money you invest in home renovation.

☐ Quality Construction

Always choose quality over quantity. Price the renovation or addition using the best-quality materials and methods of construction. If you cannot afford it, reduce the size of the project rather than compromise the quality of the job by cutting corners on construction or choosing substandard finishes. Build a smaller addition or divide the project into stages, remodelling the bathroom this year and saving the family room until you can do it exactly the way you wish.

☐ Life-Cycle Costs

Choose low-maintenance materials and methods wherever possible. While renovation can be a satisfying hobby, the joys of playing fix-it every weekend soon wear thin when the tiles loosen around the tub for the third time in two years because you continue to glue them directly to the wallboard instead of correctly setting them in a mortar bed. In this case, a little more labour at the outset buys you freedom from future repair. Oftentimes, low maintenance is simply a matter of making the right choices when planning the renovation. For instance, high-performance glass virtually eliminates the condensation that forms on most windows during the coldest part of the winter, rescuing

the homeowner from years of mopping up condensate, battling mould, repainting the sash and eventually replacing the rotted wood sills.

Low-maintenance products do not always cost more, but even if they do, paying a premium for durability is a good investment in the long run. For instance, Gene Logsdon in *The Low-Maintenance House* estimates that it costs around $4,000 to reroof 3,200 square feet with fibreglass shingles and just over $7,000 to do the job with concrete tile. On the surface, it seems more practical to choose shingles, but the opposite is true if you consider the life-cycle maintenance costs. Concrete tile lasts as long as the house, ultimately costing only $145 per year, while shingles have a life expectancy of 25 years and cost $176 annually.

☐ Labour Savings

One way to afford better-quality materials is to do the actual construction yourself, since the cost of most jobs splits equally between labour and materials. If you want to do your own renovations but have no building experience, try your hand first at something small—a playhouse for the kids or a storage shed. Not only will your skills improve with experience, but your ideas about what you want and what you think you can accomplish will also change. One advantage of renovating a house over building one from scratch is that you already have a roof over your head. You can afford to take the time to learn the skills you need to do a good job. Unlike some other hobbies that provide manual and creative satisfaction—pottery or cooking, for example—construction is relatively permanent: you cannot throw out your mistakes. They will endure for as long as the building stands or until another renovator adds his or her amateur flourishes to yours.

☐ Time-Tested Design

Most tradespeople are endowed with healthy skepticism, but do-it-yourself home renovators should also be wary of the bizarre and unconventional in building designs, materials and techniques. Although some of these may eventually prove to be answers for age-old problems that plague housing, it is better to leave the risk of experimentation to those who can afford failure. Those on a budget should stick with products and methods that have stood the test of time and designs that will not be obsolete within a decade.

A final word of warning: renovation can be addictive. An oriental proverb states that when one stops working on a house, one dies. Heiress Sarah J. Winchester took the advice to heart and sought immortality by relentlessly adding to her house. Today her rambling mansion in San Jose, California, has 160 rooms, 200 doors, 10,000 windowpanes and 47 fireplaces. One only hopes she built with low maintenance in mind.

Indoor Conversions

Project	Started/Finished	Designer/Builder	Cost	Details/Comments

One doesn't really have to be a full-fledged expert in order to build an ordinary wall in an ordinary house or to slide a plane along a board and enjoy the results. Ancients and peasants have been doing just that for millennia, piling stone upon stone and calling the result a wall. It probably never occurred to them that they had to be trained, graded and officially licensed before attempting such a complex job. Our pioneer axeman sighted along his thumb, took another pull at the jug and whacked away at the logs. I doubt if he had ever heard of a scriber, level or calipers. His crooked walls are still standing, though. And our stone walls, our patently amateur piles of rock, suit us just fine, thank you very much.

"Amateur" is a word that applies to the same sort of people in French or in English. In English, of course, an amateur is a nonprofessional, an unskilled duffer. In French, however, the emphasis is on the pleasure rather than the lack of competence. An *amateur* is one who does something for the love of it. An *amateur* builds a gable end in stone, knowing no one else will ever see it. An *amateur* chops a crude log house out of the forest, then carves a heart on a beam . . . even though it will be buried under stories of Boers and Fenians, flowered paper, fancy panels and factory-made sheets of plasterboard. He knows it's there. I know it's there. *Vive l'amateur*.

By Charles Long, from "Well-Sheltered Spirits"

Indoor Conversions

Project	Started/Finished	Designer/Builder	Cost	Details/Comments

Municipal regulations will likely affect your renovation in one way or another. Expanding or significantly altering a house usually requires a building permit, and if some of the house is to be removed, a demolition permit may also be needed. Any changes to heating, wiring, plumbing and septic systems also require a permit. This varies from one municipality to another, so call the building department or township clerk before starting work.

When you apply for a building permit, your plans are checked for compliance with building codes and zoning bylaws that spell out property use, building height, setbacks from the street and from property boundaries, side clearances between neighbours and the proportion of the property that can be covered by a house. Plumbing, heating, electrical and building inspectors will visit your house at various stages of construction to ensure that you follow the plans and meet minimum code requirements. Aside from being law enforcers, inspectors are a valuable source of free advice on the most efficient and least expensive way to do your renovation.

These regulations are often more rigidly enforced in urban and suburban areas than in rural townships and villages. Because they differ substantially across the country, only one generalization holds true: it is the homeowners' responsibility to know the legal constraints on renovating a house and to abide by them scrupulously.

Project: _____

A comfortable house is a great source of happiness. It ranks
immediately after health and a good conscience.

Sydney Smith, 1843

Project: _____

Lead was commonly used as a paint base until the 1950s, a fact that renovators should keep in mind when stripping wood floors and trim down to the natural finish that is so popular today. Drum sanding is the most expeditious way to cut through the accumulated finishes on a wood floor, but the process can be hazardous: "Lead-based paint is poisonous, and high-speed sanders create lead dust," writes Nigel Hutchins in his book *Restoring Old Houses*. "Speaking from personal experience, after twice fainting when using the process, I have become even more a devotee of the overpainted floor." Those who insist on reducing wood to its bare essentials should wear a good-quality mask and ventilate the room while sanding the floor. For wood mouldings, Hutchins recommends using a heat gun and scraper. After most of the paint is removed, apply a chemical remover liberally, wiping the wood clean with scrapers and fine steel wool. Ventilation is essential: the fumes from chemical removers can be toxic.

Would-be strippers should also be prepared for what lies beneath the paint buildup. Instead of the honey pine so savoured by old-house aficionados, there may be a hodgepodge of basswood and white pine. Decorative paint cover-ups such as stencilling and marbleizing gave interior woods an attractive facade, and woodgraining added the simulated sophistication of mahogany, bird's-eye maple and oak to plebeian species such as red pine. For the sake of human health, the historical integrity of the house and simple aesthetics, a homeowner should think twice before unmasking the deception.

Project:

Project: _____

Experience is the name everyone gives to their mistakes.　　　　Oscar Wilde

Project: _____

A human being should be able to change a diaper, plan an invasion, butcher a hog, conn a ship, design a building, write a sonnet, balance accounts, build a wall, set a bone, comfort the dying, take orders, give orders, cooperate, act alone, solve equations, analyze a new problem, pitch manure, program a computer, cook a tasty meal, fight efficiently, die gallantly. Specialization is for insects.   Robert A. Heinlein

Project:

Project: _____

The shortest way is commonly the foulest.   Francis Bacon

88

Project:

Project: _____

Project: _____

Asbestos is now recognized as a health hazard, but it was once a common building component, valued for its fire resistance. In old houses, it was often used as insulation for metal duct work, in wallboard and plaster, in shingles, floor tiles and ceiling panels and in the heat shields behind stoves and fireplaces. As they deteriorate, however, products containing asbestos shed small fibres that, when inhaled, can lodge in the lungs causing irritation and disease. It is a good idea, therefore, to check the condition of any suspect materials. If they are not visibly disintegrating and if they are not part of an air-handling system, small areas may be better left undisturbed. In some cases, the materials can be sealed to prevent shedding: the asbestos tape on heating ducts can be covered with heat-resistant foil tape, a small heat shield can be painted with heat-resistant paint, and asbestos floor tiles can be covered with ¼-inch plywood, sealed around the edges, before new flooring is laid. Sometimes there is no alternative but to remove asbestos products. Because it is so hazardous to handle asbestos, hire professionals to do the job, and evacuate the house during the process.

Metamorphosis Outdoor

Outdoor Evolutions

Project	Started/Finished	Designer/Builder	Cost	Details/Comments

Preservatives protect against the fungi and bacteria that attack most wood when it is exposed to the elements, converting cheap, common species like spruce and pine into good materials for decks, fences and play equipment.

Pressure-treated wood has the preservative—either chromated copper arsenic (CCA) or ammoniacal copper arsenate (ACA)—applied at the factory. These inorganic arsenicals have caused birth defects and cancer in laboratory animals, but studies also show that when applied to wood, they bind tightly to the fibres: they do not migrate into surrounding soil, and they are not absorbed through the skin.

Pressure-treated wood is probably more of a health risk to do-it-yourself builders than to those who lounge on the decks. Since minute amounts of preservative-laced sawdust may be inhaled or swallowed during construction, anyone sawing pressure-treated wood should wear a dust mask and work outdoors to avoid contaminating indoor air. When it is burned, treated wood releases arsine, an extremely

poisonous gas, so bury scraps or take them to an approved landfill.

Pressure-treating does not inject preservative right to the core of the wood. Drilled or cut surfaces have to be brushed with at least two coats of liquid preservative. Wear rubber gloves during these applications, avoid dripping the chemical on plants and wash thoroughly afterwards. When the project is finished, hose it down with soap and water to remove surface deposits of chemicals.

Other paint-on preservatives such as pentachlorophenol (PCP) and creosote are highly suspect from a health standpoint. PCP contains dioxins, is easily absorbed through the skin and gives off toxic vapours for as long as seven years. Read labels carefully, since wood stains often contain chemical preservatives, particularly chlorophenols.

Chemicals can be avoided altogether by building outdoor projects with naturally rot-resistant woods such as cedar and redwood. These are relatively scarce and therefore expensive, but it may be a small price to pay for peace of mind.

Outdoor Evolutions

Project	Started/Finished	Designer/Builder	Cost	Details/Comments

Sandblasting the facade of an old brick house may only temporarily restore the building to its former glory; in the long run, this type of cleaning may in fact accelerate its demise.

Brick was originally painted, not only because it was the fashion but also because it protected porous handmade masonry. A thin crust of dirt further shields the brick from temperature fluctuations. Most preservation architects agree that the patina on a brick house should be left alone unless it seriously detracts from the historical significance of the building or unless the dirt itself is causing damage. In some cases, moisture absorbed by a heavy buildup of grime can fracture the brick as it freezes and thaws, and in industrial areas, a coating of acid fallout can lead to major physical deterioration. Masonry may also be under siege by algae, lichens or pigeon feces, which cause a chemical reaction that eats into brick.

Sandblasting is only one means of cleaning a dirty facade: it can also be scrubbed with chemicals or high-pressure water. Although fast and effective, sandblasting pits the surface of the bricks, increasing the total area that is exposed to moisture and the ravages of the freeze-thaw cycle. The process produces a windstorm of dust, but chemical spraying may pose even more serious health hazards, not only for the operator but for the entire neighbourhood.

Hosing down the walls with high-pressure water is probably the safest option, although the levels used to clean commercial buildings—10,000 pounds per square inch (psi) or more—might explode the brick in a pre-1830 cottage. A pressure of 20 to 100 psi applied a foot from the wall is more appropriate for a historic surface. If the outside of a house must be cleaned, experiment first on a test patch on an inconspicuous part of the wall, and wait awhile for the effects of weathering to take their toll. Make sure that whoever does the job is knowledgeable about old materials and has adequate permits and liability insurance. As a courtesy, inform the neighbours: more than one car windshield has been irreparably etched by blowing sand.

Project: _____

The facade of a building does not belong to only those who own it but to all who behold it.

Chinese proverb

Project:

Project:

Project: _____

An outside ornamented for show and an interior that is neglected or cheap is like nothing so much as a woman in a sable coat and 98-cent underclothes.

Emily Post

Metamorphosis

Project: _____

He who digs a well, constructs a stone fountain, plants a grove of trees by the roadside, plants an orchard, builds a durable house, reclaims a swamp, or so much as puts a stone seat by the wayside, makes the land so far lovely and desirable, makes a fortune which he cannot carry away with him, but which is useful to his country long afterwards.

Ralph Waldo Emerson, 1870

Project:

Landscape Plan

Landscape Plan

Metamorphosis

Landscaping. Can it turn common earth into paradise? Here, living on our suburban lots, in our city townhouses, on our farms or simply with our dreams, we have places that are pretty enough in their own way, with their flowers and bushes and trees. Yet they are only suggestive of what we commonly think of as landscaping: groomed parks, tree-lined avenues and boulevards, topiary and hedges, immaculate, ever-blooming perennial borders designed and maintained by professionals. Intimidation comes easily. What we have is usually passable and certainly home—but it is not paradise.

Yet paradise originally meant garden. The word was used to denote many of the gardens of the Persian king Cyrus the Great, who lived in the sixth century B.C. In the words of the Greek Xenophon, "the Persian King is zealously cared for, so that he may find gardens wherever he goes. Their name is Paradise and they are full of all things fair and good that the earth can bring forth." Which sounds a little like the biblical Paradise, but quite unlike anything a gardening northerner might expect. "All things fair and good that the earth can bring forth" are the sorts of things that will simply not grow in such a climate, even had we the skill and knowledge to grow them.

But paradise has also been defined simply as "a place of rest and joy"—just one-third of which, incidentally, is set aside for "well-balanced women," according to the Koran—and virtually any garden, with the help of skilful and sensitive landscaping, can be that. What is landscaping? It is the consideration of one's piece of property as a milieu, a vista, a unit whose parts all contribute harmoniously to the whole. Landscaping is art, yet more than art. One can use many of the same principles of design, colour and balance that would be employed on an artist's canvas, but because plants are the most important elements in this medium, time, as well as space, must be considered. The landscape artist must think not only of what is, but also of what will be—a season, a year, 20 years hence. Maintenance is essential, change optional and possible at any time. The landscape has a life of its own.

Much like the other arts, landscaping has long been the subject of changing fashion, reflecting our need to be perceived as up-to-date and either controlling or working with nature. Like that of other fashions, the history of landscaping proceeds virtually hand in hand with the history of leisure time. For aeons, landscaping was affordable to those rich enough to spend time, or to hire others to spend time, doing nothing but thinking about the aesthetics of their natural surroundings. Before that, everyone was vitally concerned with controlling and working with nature simply to ensure that there would be enough food.

Although the earliest records of plant cultivation begin about 10,000 years ago, the first decorative gardens do not appear in history until around 2000 B.C. in Mesopotamia, also the rumoured location of the Garden of Eden, Paradise indeed. These gardens were formal and had religious significance, as well as acting as public relations notices for the rulers who created them. Here, plants gathered from other lands could demonstrate, in living colour, the conqueror's dominion. The Hanging Gardens of Babylon were even more impressive, resembling, it seems, a living, green ziggurat that advertised the prowess of Nebuchadnezzar, the king who likely built them around 600 B.C. Further east, the powerful message of landscaping was also used by the Emperor Wu Ti who, in his vast second-century-B.C. grounds, exhibited rare plants gathered from throughout the Orient. Bridges, streams, pavilions and man-made hills were structural elements long appreciated in such gardens, where both wealth and restraint were displayed.

Today's amateur landscape designer may be limited by time, climate, space and finances but is at liberty to choose from any of the gardening styles of the past or even to invent a new style. We can buy plants whose ancestors grew continents away or cultivars that have been bred for more interesting colour or shape, greater hardiness or disease resistance. Native plants may be used. As long as the garden is pleasant and functional, its plants suited to the designer's needs, limitations and desires, then it can be said to be properly landscaped. As Gertrude Jekyll once wrote, " . . . the best purpose of a garden is to give delight and to give refreshment of mind, to soothe, to refine, and to lift up the heart in a spirit of praise and thankfulness."

A paradise is not impossible, even for the northern gardener, in spite of the unwieldy stuff with which he or she works: a lack of expertise; a climate that too often brings frost instead of warmth, or rain instead of sun, or sun instead of rain; too little land for what one wishes to grow, or too much land for the time one can spend with it; dogs and cats and children, all bent on making a playpen of paradise; the skepticism of neighbours; the gardener's lack of patience; his or her lack of money. It is possible, nevertheless, to create "a place of rest and joy." Beauty can be gleaned from the beasts of cleared forest, shaded backyard, desert or quagmire. Beauty has, indeed, a practicality of its own. A place to relax, play games and meditate, to have picnics and pick flowers and fruit, to enjoy sun, shade and rain can be as nurturing as a garden planted only to feed the body.

Jennifer Bennett, from "In Search of Paradise"

For the Record

Maintenance
Money Matters
Sources

The strength of a nation is derived from the integrity of its homes.   Confucius

For the Record, if completed diligently, will become a kind of operating manual for your house. In these pages, you can record all the regular maintenance and repairs that are needed to keep the house in prime condition. The section opens with a list of service people who have worked on the house, what they were hired for and how much the job cost. There is also a place for comments that might prove useful in the future, such as how well the work was done, how much time it took or the tradesperson's usual busy season.

The maintenance records, pages 106 to 109, begin with a place to list the chores that must be done each spring and fall—cleaning out the gutters, retrieving the gladiolus bulbs, putting up the screens or storm windows. Use this as a reference guide to make sure the house and property are snugly battened down for the winter or ready for the summer. Some jobs, such as pumping out the septic tank or painting the outside of the house, are done every few years: make a note of these under Periodic Chores, listing how frequently each should be tended to. This page will be especially useful if you rent the house or leave it in someone else's care for an extended period of time.

Use pages 107 to 109 to keep track of irregular maintenance and repairs done to the house, inside and out, things like replacing a rotted fencepost, patching the roof, plugging a basement leak, taking the squeak out of the stairs, caulking the windows or oiling the garage doors. Because houses and families vary, this chart is blank, but you may want to divide the space with your own headings: for example, Windows and Doors, Floors, Walls, Roof, Electrical, Plumbing,

Heating and Cooling, Exterior.

Memory is surprisingly unreliable when it comes to such details, and it may prove useful to know exactly how often water in the basement was a problem or whether the shingles lived up to the manufacturer's longevity claims. Once you learn how to do something—gaining access to that recessed ceiling fixture, for instance—make a note of it, either here or on a separate piece of paper in your filing system (see Sources, page 120). It is especially important to note when pesticides were applied to the house or garden, since overexposure to these chemicals can be a health hazard. The last two pages of the maintenance section are devoted to appliances. Here, you can record your large and small appliance purchases along with their cost and warranty information. Leave a few lines between each entry and use the space to keep track of how often the machine was serviced. Any large furniture purchase that comes with a warranty—a piano, perhaps—can also be included.

The final six pages of *For the Record* are reserved for household financial data, tucked discreetly at the back of the book. Here you can record the details of the house purchase, your mortgage and the annual operating expenses of the house. The fiscal part of your chronicle closes with a place to list your family treasures. This is useful for insurance purposes, but it is also a memoir of where and how you acquired favourite paintings, antique dishes and special coins to add to your collection. Finally, the book ends with source listings of reference books you will find useful during the years you spend in your house.

Phileen Dickinson

Service People

Job	Date	Cost	Notes

Wood-burning stoves and fireplaces—even those fed with well-seasoned hardwood and plenty of air—produce creosote, a brittle black crust that clings to the walls of the flue and accumulates at the elbows, damming the flow of smoke up the chimney. Worse, if ignited by a rising ember from a roaring blaze, creosote causes chimney fires.

Pioneers often dragged a small evergreen or a gunny sack filled with sand up the flue to dislodge creosote, but a stiff brush fitted with metal rods or a weighted rope is easier and much more effective. Buy steel brushes that are exactly the same size as the chimney, or buy flexible-bristle brushes—recommended for some prefabricated steel chimneys—that are slightly larger than the flue.

Creosote dust is potentially carcinogenic, so keep it out of your lungs and your house. Wear a dust mask, and be sure the stove or chimney damper is sealed; when cleaning the fireplace flue, tape a piece of plastic over the opening into the room. Clean the chimney on a cool day and open a basement window so that there is a good updraft in the chimney to draw the dust outside. Never use a vacuum to clean up ash and stray bits of creosote: the fine particles may damage motor bearings, and some will be discharged back into the house with the exhaust.

How often the chimney is cleaned depends on the stove, the wood and how it is burned, but it is a good idea to check the chimney for creosote buildup every month during the heating season, pulling out the brushes when the creosote deposit is more than ¼ inch thick. Use a flashlight to make sure the entire length of the chimney is clean, paying special attention to elbows, joints, the damper and the spark arrester on the chimney cap.

For those who do not want to tackle the job, most areas are now served by professional chimney sweeps who will clean your flue for a nominal fee. As a bonus, according to superstition, touching the bristles of a sweep's brush, shaking his hand or giving him a quick kiss will ensure a season of good luck.

For the Record

Regular Maintenance   Spring   Fall

Periodic Chores

Maintenance and Repair Record

Job	Date	Cost	Notes

Heating, cooling and ventilating equipment should be cleaned regularly. This not only improves its efficiency but also reduces the amount of dust, bacteria and spores that blow through the house when the machines turn on. At the beginning of every heating or cooling season, thoroughly vacuum the fans, their housings and the heat exchanger or coils. Have the duct system cleaned by a professional. Every month that the furnace or air conditioner is in use, vacuum the filter and housing; replace the filters every two months. Air purifiers should also be disassembled once a month and the collectors, filters and fans cleaned thoroughly with a soft cloth moistened with a vinegar-water mixture.

In summer, clean the air conditioner coils and drip pan every week with a mixture of one cup vinegar and one gallon of water. Likewise, clean the humidifier weekly, removing the water reservoir and all parts where mould can grow; wash them down with soapy water, then soak them in a 1:16 vinegar-water bath. Unless a humidifier is cleaned regularly, the warm, damp conditions can be a breeding ground for bacteria that cause a flu-like illness known as humidifier fever.

Maintenance and Repair Record

Job	Date	Cost	Notes

Radon is a natural gas produced by decaying radium-rich rock, but when this soil gas seeps inside a house and becomes concentrated, it can be a serious health hazard. Because it is invisible, odourless and rarely causes immediate symptoms, radon often goes undetected, but good basement maintenance can help prevent the problem. Inspect all parts of the house that are in contact with the soil, parging cracks in the basement walls and floor, sealing them with a continuous air barrier and tightly caulking all service penetrations. Floor drains are a major entry route, since soil gases can seep into the drainage tile that surrounds the house. At least two companies—Dranger and NRG Saver, both in Winnipeg, Manitoba—sell floor drain covers that stop radon infiltration. Finally, if the house is well sealed to prevent heat loss, it should have a mechanical ventilation system to provide fresh air and prevent the buildup of indoor pollutants such as radon. If radon is a concern, indoor air can be tested professionally for under $50. Check for listings under ''Laboratories—Testing'' in the yellow pages of the telephone directory, or contact the provincial health and welfare department for a list of mail-order labs.

Maintenance and Repair Record

Job	Date	Cost	Notes

Fungi—small plantlike organisms that include moulds, mildew and mushrooms—are always present in the air, but in large quantities, they can cause health problems for those who are allergic to the spores. Fungi feed on building materials such as wood, paint and adhesives and multiply rapidly in warm, dark, damp conditions. Fungi can commonly be found in basements, particularly under carpets and wall coverings that trap moisture, on the inside surface of poorly insulated areas where condensation forms and around bathroom fixtures, especially in summer. Repair leaks and buy a dehumidifier for a damp basement. Exhaust fans in bathrooms, kitchens and laundry areas will also keep humidity at the ideal levels.

Do not clean fungi with a vacuum, since it will simply distribute the spores into the air. Instead, wipe them off with a borax solution, making sure that sensitive family members are out of the house during the cleanup—fungus colonies release large numbers of spores when disturbed. Scrubbing with borax will temporarily eliminate the greenish black plants, but the bloom of mould will repeatedly return until the underlying moisture problem is corrected.

Pest Control: Indoors

Pest	Location	Chemical	Dosage	Date	Result

Pesticides are commonly used to rid houses of annoying insects, yet many of the ingredients in these chemical formulas are potential health risks. Not only do pesticides irritate eyes and lungs when they are sprayed, but the residues can remain active for days, weeks and even years. In some cases, a single fumigation has triggered total allergy syndrome, a debilitating hypersensitivity to one's environment.

Given the risks, it makes sense to control pests with natural means whenever possible: prevent bugs from getting into the house, and make it uncomfortable for them to live there. Trace ants and roaches to their point of entry and seal the gap with white glue or caulking; take away their food supply by sweeping up crumbs, wiping up spills, washing dishes immediately, storing edibles in tightly sealed containers and removing garbage and compost to the outdoors. To discourage flying insects, keep screens in good repair and eliminate any successful interlopers with a flyswatter rather than a spray bomb; dry up their water supply by repairing leaky faucets, clogged drains and cracked concrete floors.

If insects invade despite these measures, use natural controls (see Sources, page 120). Sprinkle red chili powder or borax where ants enter, or plant mint around the outside of the house near the kitchen. Trap roaches and silverfish in an empty jar baited with beer and bananas and smeared on the inside edge with petroleum jelly so that the insects cannot escape. Vacuum thoroughly every day to get rid of fleas, paying particular attention to crevices and disposing of the vacuum bag after each cleaning. Speed up the process by having all the carpets and upholstery steam-cleaned: fleas cannot tolerate extreme heat.

If you must use chemical pesticides, do so with caution. Read the label carefully, and only use the chemical for its intended purpose, in the exact manner prescribed. Do not use more than the recommended dose. Avoid inhaling the fumes, and cover all food and dishes. Keep children and pets away from sprayed areas for as long as possible; fumigate just before going on holidays and ventilate the house well while you are gone. Wash well after using a pesticide and store the container safely until it can be disposed of on special collection days for hazardous household waste. Finally, to avoid spraying too often and to safeguard the health of future occupants who may be prone to environmental illness, keep a record of all pesticide applications, both inside the house and on the lawn and gardens.

Pest Control: Outdoors

Pest	Location	Chemical	Dosage	Date	Result

Termites are a considerable threat to the integrity of wood-frame houses in many parts of Canada. They do not want to move in with you; they just want to eat you out of house and home. Termites live in underground colonies and dig tunnels to their food supply, which is cellulose or wood. If dinner sits atop a concrete foundation, they build mud tunnels straight up the wall so that they can get to their food without being exposed to fresh air and daylight. These insects need a dark, damp environment and will chew through the soft grain at the centre of a piece of wood without ever breaking through the surface. As a result, termite damage often goes unnoticed until a beam suddenly gives way.

The mud veins on exposed basement walls may be the only sign that the house is infested, though an observant homeowner may notice a cluster of insect wings near a basement wall in early spring. At that time, the soil-bound colony splits. Some of the termites sprout wings, fly outdoors and, when they have found a new site, shed their wings and burrow underground again.

The most effective way of dealing with a termite infestation is to poison the soil around and under the house, creating a barrier between the colony and its food supply. This must be done by a professional exterminator and involves powerful insecticides such as chlordane, which may have human health consequences. Instead, try to prevent termites from choosing your house as a restaurant. Make sure no wood is in direct contact with the soil and cover masonry foundation walls with metal termite shields. Pile firewood and lumber away from the house and on blocks to raise it off the ground. In termite zones, any wood that touches soil should be pressure-treated; mild preservatives such as copper naphthenate protect against rot but are no defence against these voracious insects.

Every fall, inspect the outside of the house for termite tunnels. Cracks in the concrete may have mud tunnels inside, so patch these crevices as soon as you notice them. Inside the basement or crawl space, test wood that is in contact with the foundation, using a sharp knife or ice pick to poke at the joists and plates: if the point goes in more than half an inch, the wood is damaged by either termites or dry rot. Chisel out a small section: if the wood is crumbly or spongy throughout, it is probably rot; if it is hollowed out in tunnels parallel to the grain but is still sound on the outside, termites are the culprits.

Appliance Record

Item	Manufacturer	Model/Serial#	Retailer	Date	Cost	Warranty	Service
front load washer dryer				Jan '06	2297.71		

Appliance Record

Item	Manufacturer	Model/Serial#	Retailer	Date	Cost	Warranty	Service

House Purchase

Price asked _____

Price paid _____

Date of sale _____

Closing date _____

Purchased from _____

_____

Real estate agent _____

Real estate commission _____

Land transfer tax _____

Lawyer's fees _____

Other closing costs _____

_____

House Financing

Down payment _____

First mortgage: Total amount _____

            Monthly payment _____

            Interest rate _____

            Term _____

            Amortization _____

            Mortgage company _____

            Loan officer _____

Mortgage insurance company _____

Second mortgage: Total amount _____

            Monthly payment _____

            Interest rate _____

            Term _____

            Amortization _____

            Mortgage company _____

            Loan officer _____

Mortgage Prepayment Record

Date	Amount Paid	Principal Remaining	Date	Amount Paid	Principal Remaining

Annual Operating Costs   Property Taxes

Year	Assessed Value	Mill Rate	Tax

Year	Assessed Value	Mill Rate	Tax

Utilities

Year	Water	Electricity	Gas/Oil	Wood

Year	Water	Electricity	Gas/Oil	Wood

Family Treasures

Jewellery

Item	Retailer	Cost	Purchase Date	Appraised Value	Description

Furniture

Item	Retailer	Cost	Purchase Date	Appraised Value	Description

Family Treasures   Antiques

Item	Retailer	Cost	Purchase Date	Appraised Value	Description

Art

Item	Retailer	Cost	Purchase Date	Appraised Value	Description

Family Treasures

Books

Item	Retailer	Cost	Purchase Date	Appraised Value	Description

Collections

Item	Retailer	Cost	Purchase Date	Appraised Value	Description

Insurance

Policy type _____

Company _____

Policy# _____

Agent _____

Annual premium _____

Renewal date _____

Coverage _____

_____

_____

_____

_____

_____

_____

_____

Insurance often seems like laying a bet against yourself: in paying the premium, you are backing the odds that your house will be struck by lightning or thieves. As senseless as the annual payment seems when things are going well, however, insurance becomes a sound investment if your property is actually stolen or damaged.

A typical homeowner's policy usually covers the current value of your house and its contents, their worth at the time of loss. For instance, if you bought your stereo for $1,800 three years ago, and it is valued at $1,000 now, the insurance company will only pay you $1,000, even though it may cost twice that much to buy a new unit of comparable quality. For a small extra premium, you can buy an insurance policy that covers the replacement value of your property, a worthwhile investment during periods of inflation.

It is important to have the agent explain the house insurance policy carefully. It may cover your property even when it is not in your house—for instance, a purse stolen from the car or luggage lost in transit. If you travel a lot, you may want to add such a rider to your policy. You can also add riders to your policy that cover the loss of or damage to items such as contact lenses and orthodontic appliances. However, unless both the deductible and the additional premium are very low or there is a great likelihood of loss, insuring such relatively low-cost items may not make good financial sense.

You can reduce the cost of homeowner's insurance by increasing the deductible, the amount you have to pay before the insurance

company picks up the tab. The annual savings from lower premiums will likely more than offset the higher deductible should you have to make a claim. You may also be eligible for discounts on your homeowner's policy. Some insurance companies lower the premium if your house is equipped with smoke alarms, fire extinguishers or a personal security system, or if your possessions are engraved with personal identification. If the company that currently insures you does not have such discounts, shop around for one that does. Installing safety devices will not only save you money but will also improve your family's security from fire and theft.

To make a claim on your insurance policy, you have to know exactly what has been destroyed or damaged. Few people can re-create the contents of an office desk, let alone an entire house, so it is a good idea to prepare an inventory. The fastest way to record your possessions is to rent a video camera and recorder and film each room of your house, opening all cupboards, closets and drawers. Devote special attention to valuables, laying out small items like jewellery, coins or stamps on a table and scanning them slowly. Don't forget to record the exterior, the yard, the garage, the garden shed and other outbuildings. Store the cassette in a safe place, preferably in a safety deposit box, and update it periodically. Even with a video cassette, it is important to keep a written list of your valuable personal property, including when it was bought, the price and, if it has been engraved, its identification number.

Filing Facts

A Chronicle of Our House keeps a vast amount of pertinent data handy between the covers of one book, but there are still important papers that need to be stored where you can retrieve them quickly and easily—building plans, warranties and the deed, to name but a few. Every house should have a filing system to keep track of these items, one that is comprehensive yet simple and flexible enough that it will be used.

Record Savings

The kind of information you need to store falls roughly into three categories: documents dealing with the purchase of the house, invoices and notes on improvements made to it, and papers relating to things you buy for the house. Keeping track of these costs may save you money in the long run. If you can document the original price of the house and the value of improvements made to it, you will be better able to determine the accuracy of tax assessments and the true value of the residence should you decide to sell. If you sell the house at a profit, receipts for improvements will help offset capital gains taxes. In the case of things bought for the house or for the family, such as appliances or watches, the warranties will usually be void unless the receipt accompanies the complaint.

A filing system does not require a large investment: buy a small cardboard or metal filing box and a stock of files. A few dividers will also prove useful.

The Great Divide

First, figure out the general categories that cover the kinds of information you want to keep on file, and print these labels on the dividers: for example, Family Records, House Documents, House Improvements, Household Purchases. You might also want a category for Finances and another for Taxes, where you can store the files containing income tax returns and receipts for the past seven years. Within these general categories, receipts and papers are grouped under common subjects that are filed and stored alphabetically. For instance, under Family Records, you might have files labelled Birth Certificates, Life Insurance, Medical Records, Report Cards and Wills. Under Finances, you may want files for Annual Budget, Credit Cards, Investments, Personal Loans and RRSPs.

The three categories that deal specifically with your house are House Documents, House Improvements and Household Purchases. House Documents is the place to store all the papers that apply to the building itself. You will need files labelled Purchase Agreement, Mortgage, Insurance and Property Deed. If you built the house, you may have files called Building Plans, Trade Subcontracts and Inspection Reports. If the house is older, you may want a House History file.

Under Household Purchases, create a file for each major acquisition. Here, you can store the owner's manual, the bill of sale, warranty information, care or cleaning instructions, installation diagrams and repair bills. The owner's manual will be particularly appreciated if you later sell the appliance.

Project Notes

House Improvements provides a place to store all receipts and information about work done on the house. Set up a file for each project, such as Family Room Addition or Kitchen Flooring, and arrange these alphabetically. Keep everything pertaining to the job, from the carpenter's estimate to wallpaper samples for the room. You may want to make a separate file labelled Wallpaper, where you can store samples from every room of the house. Although there is no need to keep a record of general maintenance, other than what is in your *Chronicle*, you may want to start a file called Repairs, where you can keep notes about particular household tasks that you are likely to tackle again.

Set up the files as you need them, since it is impossible to determine in advance what specific subjects will be needed. Take the time to arrange the files in each category alphabetically and keep the filing box handy. If you are unsure about where to file a specific receipt, put it in the most obvious place and put a slip of paper in the other file with a cross reference: ''See File . . .'' Periodically, go through your files and throw out any that are outdated.

For insurance purposes, make an inventory of all your possessions. This can be written, photographed or videotaped. File the inventory in its own file under House Documents and update it from time to time.

Safety Deposits

The originals of such important papers as the inventory should be stored in a safety deposit box. Make photocopies for your home filing system so that you can refer to them without making a special trip to the bank. However, life insurance policies and wills should not be stored in safety deposit boxes in case the box is sealed when the holder dies. Among the things that should be kept in a safety deposit box are photocopies of wills and life insurance policies, originals of other insurance policies, property records, personal documents such as birth and marriage certificates, divorce papers, passports, an inventory of household valuables, small valuables such as jewellery and coins, and stock and bond certificates. Make a list of the safety deposit box contents and store it in a file under House Documents.

Without a good filing system, many of these important papers can be misplaced. It is worth the effort to set aside an afternoon now to design a system that will save you hours of aggravation and possibly hundreds of tax dollars in the future.

Government Publications

Government agencies publish many pamphlets and booklets that are helpful to homeowners. Some of the better ones are listed in the appropriate categories below, but it is a good idea to check to see what is currently available from your provincial, state and federal departments of housing and energy.

Construction and Renovation

Basic Wiring
Time-Life Books, 1980

Complete Do-It-Yourself Manual
The Reader's Digest Association, 1973

Canadian Wood-Frame House Construction
Available from CMHC:
Publications
Canada Mortgage and Housing Corporation
P.O. Box 9975, Ottawa, Ontario K1G 3H7

Draw Your Own House Plans
By Mike and Ruth Wolverton
TAB Books Inc., 1983

From the Walls In
By Charles Wing
Little Brown, 1979

Housebuilding: A Do-It-Yourself Guide
By R.J. De Cristoforo
Sterling Publishing Co., 1987

How To Get Your Building Plans Through City Hall
By M.C. Leaden
Intermedia Press Ltd., 1981

Illustrated Housebuilding
By Graham Blackburn
The Overlook Press, 1974

Plans, Permits and Payments
Available free of charge from the Ontario Ministry of Municipal Affairs and Housing, Queen's Park, Toronto

Renovation: A Complete Guide
By Michael Litchfield
Wiley, 1982

The Blue Thumb Guide to Working on Your House
By Bill Schultz
Chronical Books, San Francisco, 1978

The Old-House Rescue Book: Buying and Renovating on a Budget
By Robert Kangas
Prentice-Hall, 1982

The Stonebuilder's Primer
By Charles Long
Camden House Publishing Ltd., 1981

Sunwings: The Harrowsmith Guide to Solar Addition Architecture
By Merilyn Mohr
Camden House Publishing Ltd., 1985

Healthy House

Nontoxic & Natural: How to Avoid Dangerous Everyday Products and Buy or Make Safe Ones
By Debra Lynn Dadd
Jeremy P. Tarcher, Inc., 1984

The Nontoxic Home
By Debra Lynn Dadd
Jeremy P. Tarcher, Inc., 1986
Distributed by St. Martin's Press, New York

Your Home, Your Health and Well-Being
By David Rousseau, W.J. Rea and Jean Enwright
Hartley & Marks Ltd., 1988

Preservation is the process of accurately recovering the form and detail of a structure as it appeared at a particular period of time. To accurately restore an 1830 rubblestone cottage would entail ripping off the verandah and centre gable that, although added 30 years later, give it much of its charm. Rehabilitation, however, is the process of returning a property to a useful state through repair or alteration: one can make efficient contemporary use of the building—adding wiring and plumbing and other creature comforts of the 20th century— without destroying the best period details of the structure. This is a form of historical rehabilitation, but Nigel Hutchins notes another category, adaptive rehabilitation, where the building provides a shell but the interior space is entirely reconstructed to suit the needs of the occupant—for instance, dividing up the inside of a Victorian mansion to create offices or rooms in a boarding house. Canadian restoration architect Peter John Stokes said, "One must always remember—in all facets of architectural preservation—the house is the master."

House History

The Complete House Detective
By Donalda Badone
Erin, Ontario; Boston Mills Press, 1988

History Unlimited
8 L'Estrange Place
Toronto, Ontario M6S 4S7
Researches and records the history of your house in a personal Blue Book.

"Tracing the History of a House"
By Joyce N. Watson
Ontario Library Review
March 1976, pp. 82-96

Without Our Past
By Ann Faulkner
University of Toronto Press, 1977

Maintenance

*Country Plumbing: Living With a
Septic System*
By Gerry Hartigan
Alan H. Hood Publisher, 1984

Household Hints & Handy Tips
The Reader's Digest Association (Canada), 1988

*Jackie's Home Repair and Maintenance Charts:
The Basic Guide to Home Upkeep*
By Richard G. Mills
Betterway Publications, White Hall, Virginia, 1983

The Low-Maintenance House
By Gene Logsdon
Rodale Press, 1987

Rodale's Book of Shortcuts
Edited by Cheryl Winters Tetreau and Carol Hupping
Rodale Press, 1988

*The Homeowners Handbook: What You Need to Know
About Buying, Maintaining, Improving and Running
Your Home Successfully*
By Michael McClintock
Charles Scribner's Sons, 1980

*The Simon and Schuster Complete Guide to Home
Repair and Maintenance*
By Bernard Gladstone
Simon & Schuster Inc., 1984

The Straight Poop: A Plumber's Tattler
By Peter A. Hemp
Ten Speed Press, 1986

Energy and Conservation

*Home Retrofitting for Energy Savings: An
Illustrated Guide*
By Paul A. Knight
Van Nostrand Reinhold, 1981

*In the Bank . . . Or Up the Chimney? A Dollar and
Cents Guide to Energy-Saving Home Improvements*
Thomas Nelson & Sons Ltd., 1976

Keeping the Heat In
Available from Energy Mines and Resources Canada

*Movable Insulation: A Guide to Reducing Heating and
Cooling Losses Through the Windows in Your Home*
By William K. Langdon
Rodale Press, 1980

Solarizing Your Present Home
Edited by Joe Carter
Rodale Press, 1981

*The Home Water Supply: How to Find, Filter, Store
and Conserve It*
By Stu Campbell
Garden Way, Inc., 1983

*The Solar Electric House: A Design Manual for Home-
Scale Photovoltaic Power Systems*
By Steven J. Strong with William G. Scheller
Rodale Press, 1987

The North American Wood Heat Handbook
By Gordon Flagler
Deneau Publishers & Company Ltd., 1982

The Superinsulated Retrofit Book
By Brian Marshall and Robert Argue
Renewable Energy in Canada, 1981

Who repairs his gutter repairs his whole house.

Spanish proverb

Preservation and Rehabilitation

The Canadian Old House Catalogue
By John Hearn
Van Nostrand Reinhold, 1980

The Old House Doctor
By Christopher Evers
The Overlook Press, 1986

The Old-House Journal Compendium
By Clem Labine and Carolyn Flaherty
The Overlook Press, 1980

Restoring Old Houses
By Nigel Hutchins
Van Nostrand Reinhold, 1982

Restoring Houses of Brick & Stone
By Nigel Hutchins
Van Nostrand Reinhold, 1982

This Old House
By Bob Villa and Jane Davison
Little Brown, 1980

Landscaping

*Ground Covers:
A Harrowsmith Gardener's Guide*
Edited by Jennifer Bennett
Camden House Publishing, 1987

Landscaping With Herbs
By James Adams
Timber Press, 1987

*Rock Gardens:
A Harrowsmith Gardener's Guide*
Edited by Katharine Ferguson
Camden House Publishing, 1988

The Harrowsmith Landscaping Handbook
Edited by Jennifer Bennett
Camden House Publishing, 1985

The Harrowsmith Perennial Garden
By Patrick Lima
Camden House Publishing, 1987

Insect Control

*Bugbusters: Getting Rid of Household Pests
Without Dangerous Chemicals*
By Bernice Lifton
McGraw-Hill Paperbacks, 1985

*The Encyclopedia of Natural Insect and
Disease Control*
By Roger B. Yepsen
Rodale Press, 1984

General Interest

Commonsense Architecture
By John Taylor
W.W. Norton & Company, 1983

Home: A Short History of an Idea
By Witold Rybczynski
Viking Penguin Inc., 1986

House
By Tracy Kidder
Houghton Mifflin Company, 1985

Periodicals

Fine Homebuilding
The Taunton Press
52 Church Hill Road
Box 355
Newtown, Connecticut 06470

The Heritage Canada Foundation
306 Metcalfe Street
Ottawa, Ontario K2P 1S2 or
Box 1358, Station B
Ottawa, Ontario K1P 5R4
Publishes *Canadian Heritage* magazine, several newsletters and a few books, including *Tips on Home Maintenance in Canada*, which emphasizes the maintenance of heritage houses.

Canada Century Home
21 Dorset Street East
Port Hope, Ontario L1A 1E2
A magazine of heritage houses, crafts and collectibles.

The goodness of a house does not consist in its lofty halls, but in its excluding the weather.   Chinese proverb

Notes

Credits

We gratefully acknowledge the permission granted to reprint the following excerpts:

Page 8
From "The Shining Houses" published in *Dance of the Happy Shades* ©Alice Munro, 1968. Reprinted by permission of McGraw-Hill Ryerson Limited.

Page 17
From "West of the 3rd Meridian" published in *Butter Down the Well* ©Robert Collins, 1980. Reproduced with the permission of the publisher, Western Producer Prairie Books.

Page 22
From "Ghosts of Summers Past" published in *Each Moment as it Flies* ©Harry Bruce, 1984. Reproduced with the permission of the publisher, Stoddart Publishing Co. Limited.

Page 34
From "Wintering Over" published in *Wintering Over*, a collection of short stories published by Quadrant Editions, R.R. 1, Dunvegan, Ontario K0C 1J0. Reproduced with the permission of the author.

Page 80
From "Well-Sheltered Spirits" published in *The Harrowsmith Reader III* ©Camden House Publishing Ltd., 1984. Reproduced with the permission of the author and the publisher.

Page 102
From "In Search of Paradise" published in *The Harrowsmith Landscaping Handbook* ©Camden House Publishing Ltd., 1985. Reproduced with the permission of the author and the publisher.